Entrepreneur
VOICES

ON

GROWTH HACKING

The Staff of Entrepreneur Media, Inc.

Entrepreneur
PRESS

Entrepreneur Press, Publisher
Cover Design: Andrew Welyczko
Production and Composition: Eliot House Productions

This publication is designed to provide accurate and authoritative
information in regard to the subject matter covered. It is sold with
the understanding that the publisher is not engaged in rendering
legal, accounting or other professional services. If legal advice or
other expert assistance is required, the services of a competent
professional person should be sought.

Library of Congress Cataloging-in-Publication Data
    Names: Lewis, Derek, 1983- author. | Entrepreneur Media, Inc.,
      issuing body.
    Title: Entrepreneur voices on growth hacking / by The Staff of
      Entrepreneur Media, Inc. and Derek Lewis.
    Description: Irvine, California : Entrepreneur Media, Inc.,
      [2018] | Series: Entrepreneur voices
    Identifiers: LCCN 2018006339| ISBN 978-1-59918-627-6 (alk.
      paper) | ISBN 1-59918-627-6 (alk. paper)
    Subjects: LCSH: Strategic planning. | Marketing. | Electronic
      commerce. | Competition.
    Classification: LCC HD30.28 .L4939 2018 | DDC 658.4/012—dc23
    LC record available at https://lccn.loc.gov/2018006339

Printed in the United States of America
23 22 21 20 19   10 9 8 7 6 5 4 3 2 1

CONTENTS

Contents

PART III
GROWTH HACKING RELATIONSHIPS

Contents

FOREWORD BY SHAUN BUCK

Growth Hacker, TheNewsletterPro.com

Have you ever wondered what the secret sauce is behind some of the fastest-growing, most successful companies in the world?

Why are we now seeing companies start up and grow to $1,000,000, $10,000,000, or $100,000,000 in sales in record time? What is causing this phenomenon?

Oftentimes, this crazy growth is attributed to the internet. While it's obvious that the internet has played a role as a platform that has allowed companies to provide unique services and improve quality of life, the internet wasn't the driving force behind the crazy growth of these companies.

Like with any company, you don't open your physical or virtual doors and all of the sudden floods of customers flock to your business, money in hand. No, this modern-day gold rush was created by a new breed of marketers. These marketers are not simply college grads with a marketing degree looking to create the next Fortune 500 company's branded billboard. In fact, these marketers aren't even accurately described as marketers but instead as "growth hackers."

Growth hackers are a new breed of marketers who are hyper-focused on finding new, innovative, and widely successful ways to grow a company faster at increasingly lower CAC (customer acquisition costs).

Growth hackers aren't only found in large internet unicorns. At my company, The Newsletter Pro, we've used growth hacking techniques and strategies to take an offline print newsletter business (yes, you read that correctly) from a startup to one of the fastest-growing privately held companies in America. Our growth of 2,975 percent in the first three years was followed by another 1,100 percent jump the following year—and it wasn't an accident; it was hacked.

At The Newsletter Pro, we experienced crazy growth because we used growth hacking techniques and were laser-focused on getting new customers, creating success for them, and driving referrals and our overall revenue as fast as we could. In order to do that, we couldn't rely on traditional marketing to get us there. If this is the speed of growth that sounds fun to you, you're in the right place.

As you devour this book, I want you to pay close attention because you're in for a wild ride. You're going to get to hear from some of the very best growth hackers in the world. Because of the uniqueness of this subject, a large number of crazy-smart growth hackers have contributed to this book to make sure you can see the latest and greatest ideas, techniques, and home-runs that growth hackers are using today to scale companies at lightning-fast speeds. Frankly, you're not going to find a better collection of content on the subject anywhere else.

That said, I have one final thought—and it is about you.

The fact that you're reading this book tells me something about you. It tells me that you, too, have this feeling that, right now, the way marketing is being taught and executed in most companies is not the way of the future. The old—and many times outdated—techniques you learn in school or that are used by even the largest companies are not going to help you quickly grow your company. It is obvious you're not interested in the slow-growth grind of business from our parents' generation. You know the grind I'm talking about—the kind that takes years to turn a profit and you're happy with 10 percent or maybe even 15 percent year-over-year growth. No, that's not for us.

The fact that you're reading this book tells me that you're ready to take the leap into a type of business development that is fun and exciting—the type that is going to allow you to experiment with out-of-the-box techniques to find new ways to grow at speeds unimaginable a few years ago that turns dreams into reality. If I'm right about you and why you bought this book, then welcome to the club—because you, too, are a growth hacker.

NOT YOUR AVERAGE HACKING ADVICE

The word "hacking" gets a bad rap. To hack something is to break it, essentially. To hack is to cut, to slice, to chop away—sometimes using very irregular methods of doing so. By hacking, you are breaking something down and cutting away at the excess of it. As associated with computers, hacking means to modify or break into a system or software—often with nefarious intent.

Growth hacking, however, is an altogether different kind of hack. Instead of cutting away at something in the physical world (like that annoying hedge in your backyard), you are cutting away at what keeps your business from moving forward. Like a stealthy computer hacker, you are modifying your current system in new, clever, and often unconventional ways. Growth hacking is all about stripping away the excess of your business and focusing on reinventing the very nature of growth at lightning speed. It's about flipping the script and finding new ways to move ahead of your growth projections *and* your competition.

A relatively new concept, growth hacking is finally coming into its own and is one of our most-read-about topics at Entrepreneur. From harnessing the power of chaos or scaling up at lightning speed to redefining your content marketing strategy or disrupting your local business landscape, our contributors are covering tons of new ground on growth hacking. In this book, our team of writers helps you navigate the ever-changing world of growth hacking from how to invest in your growth potential to harnessing the power of out-of-the-box marketing strategies to elevate your brand quickly. You're going to read about disrupting the marketing process, orchestrating company expansion, hiring expert growth hackers, customizing the sales process, and even amping up your relationship skills—all to achieve growth at the speed of light.

You see, this book isn't about how to copy the vibe of some cool tech startup. We focus on the things that matter—proven growth techniques and approaches that result in not just swift and sustainable growth, but also in quantifiable longevity for your business that will last generations. After all, what's the point of exponential growth if you don't have a long-term plan to go with it? Our contributors know that, as do the people they look to for the latest in growth hacking advice from design titans Chip and Joanna Gaines to rap mogul Soulja Boy. All agree—it doesn't matter where you do business or what product or service you sell; it just matters that you take each opportunity for scaling up and find a way to reinvent it for the long haul.

So, be that hacker. Chip away at what your business doesn't need. Find a way to come at your plans for expansion in new and unique ways. Cut away—no, hack away—at old methods, outdated expansion plans, and passé talking points to create the growth trajectory that will take your business where it needs to be. Let's get started!

A CRASH COURSE ON GROWTH HACKING

What is growth hacking?

It's hard to pin down, but to paraphrase Supreme Court Justice Stewart: "I know it when I see it."

In the following pages, you're going to read differing definitions of growth hacking. Some are just a matter of semantics; some are

fundamentally different. Some authors talk about the different **ways to hack your** company's growth; some are more concerned **that you know why** you want to do so in the first place. In fact, **some even offer** conflicting advice.

And that's the beauty of this book.

Instead of tips and tricks from a single author, this little gem **offers advice from** dozens of perspectives: an accelerator mentor, **a cookie dough** entrepreneur, SaaS experts, and more. Instead of **trying to find** common ground, we have found great content on **the topic and brought** it all together in one place.

Here in Part I, you'll find a cross-section of expert advice on **growth hacking** from trying to define it to trying to do it. You'll **find entrepreneurs** who love the idea and those who abhor the **phrase itself.**

Enjoy your ringside seat.

1

GROWTH HACKING IS ALL IN YOUR HEAD

Andrew Medal

For companies looking to grow, a solid growth hacker can easily be mistaken for a superhero.

With new channels through social media, video, and content popping up all the time, "hacking growth" has become a more complicated process than it was a few years ago. The game has gotten harder, but the rewards have also gotten bigger. If you have a knack for marketing and love making things go viral, there's never been a better time to become a growth hacker.

To help give you a better understanding of what it takes to be a true growth hacker, here's what you need to get you started:

1. A Feel for the Audience

The internet is packed with options that help improve conversion rates and build loyal followings. From social media pages, advertising platforms, and emails, as a hacker you have plenty of ways to cultivate a community of customers. It's your job to discover which customer segment is the most viable for your business and how you can find a way for that segment's involvement with your company to go viral.

Get started by having a feel for your audience and your ideal buyer personas. This understanding will be a good place to start, especially as you work to find out which channels your core customers will most likely be found on. Segment your audience into three to six different personas based on who you want to target first and who you want to put on the backburner.

Remember, one of the easiest ways to hack growth is to master the marketing funnel of a small niche group, and then replicate it. If you look at most tech companies that have gone viral (Facebook, Uber, Airbnb), they all follow that same mentality to some degree.

This will allow you to dissect the groups most inclined to your brand. A deeper insight into customers' interests, values, and occupations are will help you tailor your message directly to them, making it much easier to get conversions.

2. A Measurement Obsession

Today, marketers use analytics tools because they have to. Simply put, if you aren't analytics driven, you aren't a real growth hacker. Data-driven marketing tools encourage not only growth hackers but the entire organization to plan ahead and think about their results and goals in defined, measurable metrics.

Without measurement tools, marketers quickly fall victim to making decisions based on vanity metrics. Planning ahead and using solid data and management tools will help you decide which metrics are right and allow you to take action faster, smarter, and more effectively. It'll also improve the output of your team and give very clear definitions of the deliverables and goals you need to hit.

But before you go on a marketing tool buffet, it's important that you spend most of your time understanding what the right data is for your measurement model. To start, identify your business objectives, your goals for your objectives, your key performance indicators for each goal, and finally the segment audience for each objective.

The mindset behind gathering this information stems from a need to keep a focus on business goals as opposed to just one aspect of your business, like your website. As your site grows, the allure of vanity metrics can lead you away from the reason behind building your site in the first place. Your best approach to staying up to date on all of these important aspects is keeping an equal eye on your entire marketing funnel and then pinpointing which part of the funnel is the bottleneck to going viral for your company.

3. A Mind for Data-Driven Decisions

The number-one thing on every growth hacker's mind has to always be metrics. As a hacker, you will have to make decisions backed by hard data. The old fogeys of the marketing world dodge necessary analytics tools and make decisions based on gut feelings. They overlook the fact that in today's ever-changing digital age, gut feelings don't accurately reflect the actual moving parts behind your business's performance.

They rely on what they see instead of what is actually happening. On the contrary, good growth hackers understand that data-driven information will lead to a true understanding of the effectiveness of their spending. The best growth marketers understand that the best decisions and projects ride on the support of solid data.

Always have hard data to back your decisions. Start by becoming a pro at Google Analytics and work your way to new platforms from there. Growth hacking, in reality, is more a mentality than an actual skill set.

If you're obsessed with growth and a bit of a data nerd, you're already well on your way to becoming a true growth hacker.

FIVE GROWTH HACKING MYTHS FOR SOFTWARE ENTREPRENEURS

Matthew Capala

"Growth hacking" has become a popular buzzword used by many people who often know a fair amount about growth but usually very little about hacking. Certain misunderstandings and even myths have become attached to the term. These common myths are problematic because they conflate, confuse, and practically destroy the proper meaning of "growth hacking" altogether. Below are five you should be especially wary of.

1. There Is a "Growth Blueprint"

There is no ultimate blueprint, road map, template, checklist, or rulebook to growth hacking. While examples such as Airbnb, Uber, Dropbox, etc. provide nice case studies to list in blog posts, more often than not, successful growth hacking strategies and tactics work once—and only once.

The good news, however, is that there's no shortage of growth hacking best practices. You can discover them by perusing articles posted in the Growth Hacking section of Entrepreneur.com, over at GrowthHackers.com, or a via a gaggle of recent books on the subject.

Bottom line: growth hacking is as much about attitude (curiosity, playfulness, and empiricism) and capability (willingness to code and to get one's hands dirty, experiment, fail, adapt, and reiterate) as it is about replicating the methods already used in specific instances.

2. They Will Come Just Because You Built It

While it's not theoretically impossible for a great software startup to go from zero to infinity on the basis of its organic marketing efforts alone, the odds of this happening materially diminish each day as the massive user platforms (I'm looking at you,

Facebook) continue to constrict organic reach in order to attain their own growth metrics.

In the early days of the web, it was much easier to build scale, to rank on the front page of Google, or to just stand out in the feed. Today, do you really expect your world-ruling app to stand out in the app store without some kind of marketing push? Or to dominate Google by "outsourcing your SEO"? I didn't think so.

My point here isn't that attempting to build products with built-in users isn't obsolete. But unless you've got some kind of marketing budget in place to strategically push your product, you'll be running handicapped in a very competitive race. Remember, you're competing with a wily group of growth hackers!

3. Great Products Sell Themselves

This myth is likely an unwanted, unconscious byproduct of the feature-obsessed, engineering focus of so many software startups today. Yes, we know your code is beautiful. But even the best, most innately viral software needs to be discovered. Otherwise, the dream of deploying a "perpetual motion conversion machine" will remain in your head.

Discovering what will make you discoverable means digging into your data. The uglier it is, the more likely that it will yield insights.

Resources include:

- Website analytics (Google Analytics)
- Email open/click rates (MailChimp, AWeber)
- Social and content marketing (Buffer, Buzzsumo)
- SEO (SEMrush, Moz Open Site Explorer, Yoast)
- Heat maps, feedback polls, surveys, user session recording (Hotjar, Qualaroo, Inspectlet, ClickTale)

Measure this data, analyze what's working, and then optimize. Repeat as necessary.

4. Growth Hacking Isn't "Black Hat"

"Black hat" refers to aggressive, often under-handed SEO strategies. Yet just because your strategies and tactics are incomprehensible to your standard Wharton-educated CMO, that doesn't make them disreputably black hat. (If there's anything truly "black hat" and flat-out illegal, it's the way Madison Avenue agencies habitually—allegedly—use media rebates from big brand budgets to line their own pockets.)

Sure, growth hacking often means using legal loopholes (Uber), reverse engineering (SEO), algorithmically generated anti-competitive tactics (Google), and other tactics that may or may not be entirely ethical. But these tactics are part and parcel of the envelope-pushing hacker ethos, which doesn't wait for a tactic to be validated by the establishment before it's deployed.

5. It's All About Acquiring New Users

Fred Wilson, a veteran New York-based VC who knows a thing or two about startup culture (Wilson's firm survived the dotcom bust of 2000 very nicely), notes that too many businesses these days are stepping on the gas before they find a proven product-market fit. Instead, Wilson suggests that a company "focus on your 90-day retention numbers and make sure to nail them and prove you have a product market fit. Then scale."

Growth hackers know that existing users are always the best place to look for new users. Uber's strategy reflects this stance perfectly. It's all about personal referrals, word of mouth, and unpaid referrals. Put another way, "Leaky buckets don't need more water; they need their holes fixed." This means that a lot of growth hacking isn't that radical or revolutionary; it's about paying attention to what your best customers want, then giving them more so they'll serve as trusted, reliable PR mouthpieces.

Do the Work

Andrew Chen—one of the first to really define growth hacking—suggests that action and experimentation lie at the essence of the term. Unless you're actively probing, testing, learning, optimizing, and failing, you're just "talking the talk."

Chen put it nicely in a Reddit "Ask Me Anything" session. "People," he wrote, "are getting all their knowledge about growth from reading blogs, rather than actually doing the work, running the experiments and building great products."

I couldn't have said it better.

3

THE ENTREPRENEUR'S GUIDE TO HIRING A KICKASS GROWTH HACKER

Neil Patel

So you've heard of growth hacking and you want it. If you're an entrepreneur, you'd be crazy not to want it. "Growth? Hacking? Heck, yes! I'll order three of those, please!"

Unfortunately, growth hacking is often misunderstood. The word "growth" is undeniably positive and "hack" is a buzzword. But what we're left with is an emotionally appealing word without a whole lot of substance

So, how do you hire a growth-hacking ninja who will skyrocket your startup to the top?

Understand What It Is . . . and Is Not

To wrap our heads around the concept, here is the definition from Wikipedia:

> *Growth hacking is a marketing technique developed by technology startups which use creativity, analytical thinking and social metrics to sell products and gain exposure.*

In other words, it's in marketing where you are free to color outside the lines. Gone are the marketing conventions of *Mad Men*. Replacing the old approaches are a slew of social media-oriented and Internet-powered techniques combined with other mystical ingredients that together make up today's digital marketing milieu.

Yes, growth hacking is all of that and more. But don't let techniques throw you off. Growth hacking isn't all technique. Growth hacking is a mindset—a way of approaching the whole idea of marketing. Sean Ellis, the man who coined the term defined it as "a person whose true north is growth."

That definition says nothing about techniques.

That's why I want to emphasize growth hacking as a mindset—a focus rather than a set of systems.

Growth hacking requires outside-the-box thinking: skepticism toward conventional marketing methods, plus the ability to pivot and adapt to new situations.

So, how exactly do you find the perfect person who possesses all of these characteristics?

Look for a Strategist—Not a Technician

You want to find someone who is a master of strategy rather than actual technical implementation.

Let me illustrate. One growth hacking technique is split testing (a method of conducting controlled experiments to improve a website). You could do one of two things:

1. Hire a conversion optimizer who is skilled at split testing.
2. Hire a growth hacker who tells you to do split testing . . . but who may not personally be able to do it.

See the difference?

The growth hacker knows that you need split testing in order to have a website that is optimized for conversions. The conversion optimizer knows how to do the split testing and how to implement the winning variation.

Strategists can pull together all the different pieces of marketing and growth, synthesizing them into a powerful force that allows you to grow at a ridiculous rate. They may not know the nitty gritty of every piece, but they recognize the importance of every piece and how they work together.

Don't Look for a Growth Hacker

Here's a classic rookie mistake. An entrepreneur wants a "growth hacker." So, they prance off to Craigslist or LinkedIn to find one. But hold up a sec.

Remember, growth hacking is a mindset. It's not a job description. It's an approach to marketing. If someone calls themselves a "growth hacker," they may or may not indeed be a growth hacker. In some cases, they may completely misunderstand growth hacking altogether.

Rather than look for a "growth hacker," seek out a really good marketer who possesses a growth hacking focus.

Find Someone Who's Done It Before

The best growth hackers are those who have hacked growth before. This should be obvious. Unfortunately, it's easy to get swept up in the hype, the verbiage, and the visions of exploding growth. When that happens, you can overlook the basic qualifying feature of the growth hacker: have they done it before?

Sean Ellis became the consummate growth hacker of Silicon Valley when he discovered the power of disruptive marketing. He was able to think beyond techniques to truly analyze the characteristic aspects of a business. And he got results. He didn't have a playbook he could hand off to a "marketing guy." Instead, he created systems and processes that could be scaled and maintained to channel torrents of growth into a business.

Can you hire Sean Ellis? Yes, kind of. But the more important thing is to find someone who has a few notches in their marketing belt—innovative approaches to marketing that have produced bottom-line results.

Become a Growth Hacker Yourself and Hire Specialists

One of the most direct routes to finding a kickass growth hacker is to be one. How, you ask?

At this point, it's become a mantra in this article, but I will reiterate it. Growth hacking is a mindset. It's not a set of sexy techniques. It's not a method. In fact, growth hacking can get wild and out of control. Why?

Because it's a mindset. Growth hacking is fueled by an insatiable desire to grow, come hell or high water. Growth hacking stops at nothing to achieve the goal of growth. Growth hacking rests on trial and error, sometimes to the point of losing touch with reality. But that's kind of the whole point.

Growth hacking doesn't come with a how-to guide. Growth hacking feeds off innovation. So, here's how to begin your personal transformation into a growth hacker:

- *Understand marketing at a foundational level.* I'm not talking about methods. I'm talking about the entire approach of marketing. You must know your customers and your market, and understand data.
- *Discover what's working.* Become familiar with growth-hacking techniques that have worked for other startups. Read about the growth sagas of Airbnb, Dropbox, and Uber, and to learn how they did it.
- *Innovate. Create. Test.* You'll find your greatest successes come from just trying stuff. As Sean Ellis wrote, "Since most growth ideas fail, it becomes critical to test a lot of them. The faster you can hack together an idea, the sooner you can start testing it for some signs of life."

Conclusion

The minute you think you understand growth hacking is the minute you forget what it is. Don't worry; you're in good company. Growth hacking is an elusive concept. Nobody owns a definition. Just as there's no single correct definition, so is there no single right profile for the ideal growth hacker. There are no lists of qualifications, years of experience, or types of software a growth hacker needs to know.

You'll know your growth hacker when you meet them. They'll be wild-eyed talking about growth and passionate about innovation. They will be experienced in the art and ready to make a positive impact on your business.

TO GROW A BUSINESS, EXPECT SOME CHAOS

Andrew Leonard

Dan Lewis has been wrestling with one of the most common and critical bottlenecks that bedevil every tech startup seeking to scale fast: How can his company staff up quickly enough to cope with expected growth without blowing through cash unsustainably? Lewis is the CEO and co-founder of Convoy, an on-demand trucking startup headquartered in Seattle, so the first idea he had felt obvious: He should open up a second office in a city that's way cheaper than Seattle.

But he just wasn't sure. Which is why, on a Friday evening in early March, he'd trekked down to Silicon Valley to meet a man known to have answers to quandaries like this: Reid Hoffman.

The two men sit down at the Sand Hill Road offices of Greylock Partners. Greylock, where Hoffman is a partner, led a round of financing for Convoy in early 2016. Hoffman now sits on the company's board.

"So, what shall we talk about today?" he asks. "Customers or recruiting?"

"Recruiting," Lewis answers.

Lewis dives into the details of his problem, and Hoffman settles into a posture that looks well-used. He steeples his hands in front of his chin, fingertips almost touching his lips, elbows splayed sharply to the left and right. His eyes might be half-closed, but his body language is benevolent; he could not possibly be more attentive.

And when Lewis is done, Hoffman has plenty to say. If Convoy *does* pursue a second office, they'd better make sure direct flights are available from the new city back to Seattle. Requiring execs to regularly make multiple-stop cross-country journeys plays hell with company culture. It's a minor point, but one you might never think of unless you'd been there yourself.

But splitting up corporate teams may be premature, Hoffman adds. It runs the risk of disrupting "the learning loop"—that all-important, constantly iterating process in which a startup figures out how best to do whatever it's doing by observing itself in action and making the necessary course adjustments.

Lewis nods. You can see him writing those words down in his mind: the learning loop. This, after all, is the effect Hoffman has on people. It's why the 49-year-old billionaire, co-founder of LinkedIn, veteran of PayPal, and venture capitalist, is widely considered something of a seer in Silicon Valley who can distill complex ideas down to important truisms. For founders wrestling with big, sticky questions about their companies' promise and direction, a few words from Hoffman can go a long way. A conversation can go even further.

That's why Lewis and his co-founder chose Greylock as their lead investor. "Reid can go into the weeds and say, 'Here is how to think of an onboarding experience for a product, here's how to think of a marketplace, here's how to think of a recruiting growth strategy," Lewis says later. Another beneficiary of Hoffman's capital and wisdom, Kiva president Premal Shah, concurs: "Reid gets in the foxhole with you."

But for Hoffman, getting into weeds and foxholes isn't just about helping the individuals he's invested in. It's about something greater—something that, he hopes, will push all entrepreneurs to grow their companies strongly and smartly. It's about nurturing an adaptable mindset suitable for navigating a confusing, chaotic world. All in the hope of making that world better for everyone.

Born in Palo Alto, raised in Berkeley, educated at Stanford and Oxford, Reid Hoffman is a very smart guy. He originally wanted to be a philosopher, but he also wanted to have a concrete impact on the world, and eventually he concluded that abstract reasoning in academia wasn't going to give him the scale to get him or the world to where it needed to be. In the mid-'90s in Silicon Valley, the lure of the digital revolution was irresistible. He got the lay of the land from gigs at Apple and Fujitsu and in 1997 started his first company, a primitive social networking operation called SocialNet.

SocialNet failed, but Hoffman recalls the experience as invaluable. After SocialNet, Hoffman joined his college friend Peter Thiel on the board at PayPal, where he soon became the COO and then executive vice president. eBay's subsequent purchase of PayPal in 2002 for $1.5 billion made Hoffman a multimillionaire. He began investing in startups and co-founded LinkedIn in 2003. He joined Greylock in 2009. In 2016, Microsoft purchased LinkedIn for a whopping $26 billion. (Hoffman joined Microsoft's board of directors in March.) Among the startups he has helped mentor are Airbnb, Mozilla, Zynga, and Groupon. Greylock declined to provide details on Hoffman's current net worth, but after the sale of LinkedIn concluded, *Forbes* calculated it at $3.7 billion.

But a funny thing happened on the way to billionaire-dom. Reid Hoffman, capitalist par excellence, ended up becoming a philosopher anyway. He has written two books—*The Startup of You* and *The Alliance*—and is working on a third, *Blitzscaling*, which is an adaptation of a course he taught at Stanford with Greylock partner John Lilly. All three drop heavy doses of knowledge on how to form the proper entrepreneurial mindset. Hoffman's philosophy is based on the principle that entrepreneurship is a force for good. He is convinced that in the long run, more Silicon Valley-style innovation will lead to greater prosperity and more jobs. "The world's better off the more Silicon Valleys there are," he says, "and the more scaled companies there are."

So how do you scale a company?

That's where it gets interesting.

Premal Shah first met Reid Hoffman at PayPal. In 2006, after Shah joined Kiva, a nonprofit that crowdsources microloans to people around the world, he recalls chasing Hoffman down in a parking lot hoping to get his one-time colleague to invest in the nonprofit. Before Shah could utter a word, Hoffman said, "The answer to your question is yes."

Hoffman not only invested but also joined the board and has stayed there ever since. Kiva's innovative technology platform helps would-be entrepreneurs across the world get funding. That meshes perfectly with Hoffman's desire to encourage entrepreneurial productivity—and he believes big platforms can connect people in important ways.

Plus, even nonprofits need to scale. Shah remembers back in 2012, when Hoffman began hammering that point in board meetings. Kiva was doing reasonably well by nonprofit standards and distributing millions of dollars, but Hoffman wasn't satisfied. During one meeting, Hoffman observed that "one of the problems with Kiva is that you actually have to pay money to participate."

There's a joke in here: Only in Silicon Valley, land of hyperinflated values for companies that make zero profit, would a hugely successful businessman and venture capitalist point out that the act of charging customers could be construed as a bad business model. But there was method to this particular bit of madness. No one has to pay to use LinkedIn or Facebook or Gmail, which is why the masses will give them a shot. When a curious person arrived at Kiva, though, the only thing to do was give money—and even if you were reasonably confident that your $25 loan to a motorcycle repairwoman in Uganda would eventually be paid back, you still had to get past that initial credit card plunge. There was friction in the system.

Hoffman came up with a new strategy, a "freemium" model in which Kiva would just plop down a pile of cash and let its users decide where to loan it. And he put his own money down—$1 million—to test the theory that Kiva could bootstrap its growth by jump-starting loaning activity.

"We said, 'Hey, lend out Reid Hoffman's money. Do good for free,'" recalls Shah. "We just wanted to see what would happen."

What happened is that 50,000 people joined Kiva in one month (a huge jump over the normal 10,000) and then those new members ended up loaning out an additional three million of their own dollars. Hoffman made back most of his donation, while setting an example that was quickly followed by Google and Hewlett-Packard, who established similar philanthropic programs for all their employees.

The Kiva example nicely illustrates some themes that Hoffman has stressed. Take chances, learn from your experiences, and be ready to pivot. But it also sheds light on why Hoffman is currently so focused on the question of scale. It's not enough to just have a good idea and get a little traction. Real change requires a more ambitious canvas.

"People are still very focused on the startup story: risk-taking founders, with a bold idea, some capital, and a network supportive environment go out and take the shot on goal," says Hoffman. "But the problem is this is no longer the truth about what makes Silicon Valley so special. There are lots of places that have technical universities, venture capital, bright young talent, and even relatively risk-taking cultures, because everyone has realized, oh, wow, taking that risk actually can be valuable. But what they haven't realized is that that's only the first step—that what is really critical for making these companies go is scale."

So, what's the second step toward getting to scale?

"Expect chaos," he says.

But beneath all the operational aspects involved in scaling a company lies something more fundamental. Hoffman believes a successful entrepreneur must be flexible, ready to adapt, and willing to accept that although the future is essentially unknowable, there is always something new to find out.

"One of the first things that you learn when you are trying to do scale at speed," says Hoffman, "is to focus on your learning loops."

The simplest way to define learning loop is as a process in which your goals are constantly modified by experience. One of the worst mistakes a startup entrepreneur can make is to stick blindly to plan A when market realities are telling you it is way past time to go to plan B. Hoffman has done a lot of thinking about pragmatic ways to enhance learning loop efficiency.

"It's all about 'OODA,'" he explains.

I look blank.

"Observe, orient, decide, act. It's fighter pilot terminology," says Hoffman. "If you have the faster OODA loop in a dogfight, you live. The other person dies. In Silicon Valley, the OODA loop of your decision-making is effectively what differentiates your ability to succeed."

The critical point Hoffman is always trying to get across—in his books, his podcasts, his interviews with journalists, and his mentoring sessions with company founders—is that no one really knows what is going to happen next. Rare indeed is the business plan that survives contact with reality intact.

Examples from his own career come readily to mind.

Exhibit A: PayPal. PayPal, says Hoffman, spent two years perfecting a technology that allowed PalmPilot users to make mobile payments. As a sideline, it also worked out a simple system for making payments via email; at the time, the company thought of that as a patch for when a PalmPilot user and a non-PalmPilot user wanted to split the bill for a meal.

The service launched, and after a week, says Hoffman, executives discovered that almost no one was making mobile transactions with their PalmPilot. But there was a hubbub of activity on eBay of people using the email payment feature to pay for their bids. As Hoffman remembers, there was some preliminary discussion of whether or not the company should quash the eBay activity; some saw it as an unlooked-for distraction from their primary business plan.

"We have all this PalmPilot technology," says Hoffman, "and this is the thing that makes us cool, and then, at the end of the week, we're like, 'No, no—these are our customers.' It's actually, in fact, the email payments on eBay that matter!"

Today, when company founders are seeking Greylock's funding, Hoffman and his partners will look for signs of learning loop capacity. They want to see whether the founder can adjust and adapt on the fly when presented with new information or advice. Greylock is fine with funding a company that might not have the clearest idea of how it will make money. But funding an entrepreneur who is too rigid— who can't go with the flow of whatever the market dictates—is an absolute nonstarter.

Hoffman has a name for the mindset of the successful entrepreneur (of course). He calls it permanent beta. There is no such thing as a permanently finished product, even inside your own head; everything is always a work in progress. "It's basically feeling that you always need to be learning," he says. "That you know things but don't know the whole game, and you are alert to how the game is changing."

He dives into this in more detail in *The Startup of You*:

The conditions in which entrepreneurs start and grow companies are the conditions we all now live in when fashioning a career. You never know what's going to happen next. Information is limited. Resources are tight. Competition is fierce. The world is changing. And the amount of time you spend at any one job is shrinking. This means you need to be adapting all the time. And if you fail to adapt, no one—not your employer, not the government—is going to catch you when you fall.

Everyone, in other words, needs to be their own fighter pilot.

"It's an intense amount of work, and you are going to have to move fast," he says. "You've probably heard me say that entrepreneurship is throwing yourself off a cliff and assembling an airplane on the way down. Well, the ground is coming, and you have to be comfortable cooperating while you are fearful of vertigo. Even if you are energized by it, the easiest way to be able to function well in that environment is to be something of an adrenaline junkie."

But what if you're not an adrenaline junkie?

As a lover of philosophy, Hoffman may appreciate that he's creating something of a paradox. In interviews and across his books, he repeatedly points out that the qualities of successful startup founders are also the qualities that can help anyone inside any career. We live in an era of destabilization, he argues. Nothing anywhere is predictable, which means we're all better off living in permanent beta.

And yet, isn't it fair to say that the disruption caused by Silicon Valley startups—and to some degree, by Hoffman himself—is itself a source of at least some of the destabilization? What are people who aren't adrenaline junkies and don't feel comfortable jumping off cliffs supposed to do when their jobs disappear because a new app has upended yet another industry?

"I think most people don't react well to uncertainty," he concedes when I put this to him. "And that is part of the reason you have fear and the renewed rise of strongman politics around the world."

But is Silicon Valley culpable for all the negative things in the world?

Hoffman isn't sold on that. While our ever-changing economy may be difficult today, it's not at all clear that it's a permanent condition. And while he acknowledges that the negative job impact of developments like self-driving cars and trucks "will be one of the very big bumps along the way," he doesn't believe that artificially intelligent robots will take all our jobs. New conditions create new opportunities—the openings that entrepreneurs will use to build companies that scale become important and help everyone around them. Education is a good example, he says. What if, he suggests, instead of packing dozens of students into classrooms or hundreds into lecture halls, we could move to a system where there was a teacher for every three students? That becomes a sector with *more* jobs—not fewer.

"There are a lot of professions that could actually grow as work is redistributed," he suggests. "During the agrarian-to-industrial revolution, there was obviously turbulence in the middle, too, but the long-term story was good."

Making sure that the long-term story has as happy an ending as possible is Reid Hoffman's goal, a point underlined by his activism, his philanthropy, and his decision to spend as much time as he can sharing his ideas and experience to help companies grow while the ground shifts beneath their feet. And that's what Hoffman, the philosopher king of entrepreneurs, has dedicated himself to doing. Here's the upgrade path, he says. Here's how you tweak your learning loop.

Expect chaos, he says, and then go from there.

HOW ACCELERATORS CAN HELP OR HURT YOUR STARTUP

Yaov Vilner

Besides my day job, I spend many hours each month mentoring young startups in accelerators across London, Berlin, Tel Aviv, and the U.S.

I find it fulfilling to absorb the energy in these platforms even when I don't really have time; it inspires me. However, many startups make some common mistakes in their early stages. Choosing the wrong acceleration program or mentors can cause long-term damage.

Here are a few lessons I'd like to pass on.

Don't Be Swayed by Big Names

Don't be tempted to sign up for an accelerator simply because a major brand is behind it. Ensure you have all the relevant information about the portfolio of the potential accelerator and the mentors who will be involved before choosing the one that's most suitable for you.

It's true that a major corporation can open doors with respect to client access or even minor funding, but as the saying goes: You can only make a first impression once. There is only one chance in your pre-seed phase, and you must make sure that these perks are all relevant to your startup's success and unique direction.

And don't plan your business strategy around those big names. While being part of an accelerator may give you a foot in the door with them, that doesn't mean you can count on their business. Your long-term success shouldn't be based on working with any one company. Focus on the fundamentals of your business, and use the accelerator to make your plans happen faster . . . but your plan should work regardless of whether you're in an accelerator or not.

Focus on Focus

Speaking of focus, your young startup only needs one thing that isn't always seen as a priority by all accelerators program managers: focus. You should always aim to know exactly what your product is trying to change in the world and who your audience is.

It would be a mistake to count only on the marketing coach inside the program to help you, as you never know if his vision is narrow or wide. An ex-CMO of a fintech startup, for example, will have great insight regarding financial startups, but a founder of a marketing agency can have insight about more verticals.

Make sure the mentoring sessions offered by the accelerators will be tailor-made to fit your needs. If the program doesn't have everything you need—and what program does?—don't be afraid to look beyond the in-house resources you have available.

Start Planning Your Hiring

While in an accelerator, your startup probably consists of you and a co-founder. You'll quickly learn that your entire product will rise and fall on the staff members behind it—and in an accelerator, that's the program staff. They're the ones helping you build it, shape it, and spread the word about it.

But just because you already have a team of people you can rely on, don't wait to start planning on hiring your own people. I've seen too many accelerator participants wait until they absolutely need to hire someone before putting thought into it. You can never start planning too early for who you need on your team.

When you're ready to hire your first few team members, though, the program staff and its partners are some of the best networks to tap. Because they're already familiar with your startup and your personality, they have a good perspective on what you need and how you work. You can multiply the number of good candidates—and therefore the odds of landing the perfect fit—by leveraging their networks.

Don't Be Afraid to Leave

If you rise to stardom too fast, don't hesitate to leave the program early. As much as I am a big fan of startup accelerators, they should adapt to you more than you adapt to them.

If your startup is going viral and you feel the time has come for massive hiring and funds, don't lose that momentum simply because you still have a couple of months to go in your current program. Even if you feel uncomfortable telling your accelerator program manager about dropping out, don't let your company's success stop you from doing what's best. They're there for you—not the other way around.

Accelerator programs are there for a reason: to accelerate the growth of your business. Use them as an initial push to build a strong base for your startup. If the time is right, empower yourself and don't hesitate to leave early to fly on your own. Your main focus should always be your business, and the best accelerators understand this and will encourage you to do just that.

You may not think this will be a problem. However, it may mask a deeper problem: being afraid to leave the nest. It's one thing to have an immediately accessible group of people and mentors who want to see you succeed, free office space, and the comfort of working inside a ready-made environment. That's part of the idea behind accelerators: they make it easy to get started.

But if they've done their job, you've grown without having to create much of the infrastructure, workflows, and other details that usually accompany that growth. Leaving the accelerator and having to create what you've taken for granted from the ground up can be challenging. But if you've outgrown the nest, then you're only hurting your company by staying there.

ENTREPRENEUR VOICES SPOTLIGHT: INTERVIEW WITH MATTHEW POLLARD

author of **The Introvert's Edge**

When we hear "growth hacking," we immediately think of Silicon Valley tech titans. These companies' exponential growth is the stuff of venture capitalists' dreams. But growth hacking isn't limited to digital platforms. Any business can experience serious growth, be they an international manufacturer or an independent service professional. "Growth" is whatever growth looks like for that business.

Matthew Pollard, author of *The Introvert's Edge* and known as the "Rapid Growth Guy," works with businesses of all kinds: telecoms, morticians, tech companies, appliance manufacturers, real estate firms, financial institutions, and solopreneurs to help them achieve rapid growth. His approach doesn't rely on reengineering your products or spending millions on your IT infrastructure, but on achieving clarity in purpose and pursuit.

Entrepreneur: You shy away from the term "growth hack." Why?

Pollard: A lot of people claim to be "growth hack experts," but when you look at what they do, you see that they're just utilizing a new tactic—Facebook ads or LinkedIn prospecting, for example—to help businesses grow their market. While I might embrace these tools in my own business, you don't start with tactics. These things might work in the short-term, but at some point, other companies start adopting the technique and its effectiveness will level out or even fade out altogether. I can't tell you how many "growth hackers" I've seen charging thousands of dollars to teach a specific tactic that I know has already lost its usefulness.

I mean, think about websites 10 or 15 years ago. At that time, having an online presence could be a major differentiator. Today, everybody has a website. It's the cost of doing business.

When looking at growth hackers' advice, I always ask, "Could the success they're pointing to be recreated today without that specific technology?" If the answer is no, then what they have is a short-term hack. That's only going to be effective as long as other competitors don't adopt it.

I don't start with short-term hacks. They have their place, but I want to find strategies that will allow rapid growth in the long-term regardless of the tools I use to implement those strategies along the way.

Entrepreneur: Where do you start with strategy?

Pollard: To seriously grow your business in a sustainable manner, disregard whatever tactics your competition uses. You need to first identify the business you're in and, more importantly, what drives you and your team. Before you try to seriously grow your business, you need to know why you're growing or if it's even the right way—to make sure the ladder you're climbing is leaning against the right wall, as Stephen Covey says.

The first thing to do is to list the goals for your business. You would be amazed at how many founders and CEOs have never gone through the process of figuring out where they're really going with the business. Their sales teams may have quotas or their executive team may have a growth target, but there's not much alignment between their tactics and those numbers.

When working with large teams, the first step is to create three business goals. When I'm working with an entrepreneur or a firm's founder, the first step is to write down three business goals as well as three personal goals—and one of those personal goals has to be entirely selfish. By that, I mean that it's simply something you want and you don't have to justify or explain why you want it; it's just something that will drive you.

Especially with high achievers, that exercise goes pretty quickly. The second step is to write down in 250 words or less why each of those goals is important. For teams, this is where they start getting into the "why" of what they do and the real aim of the company. For individuals, this exercise can be life-changing: when they begin to explain why they want a certain achievement, they start digging into what truly motivates them at a deeply personal level.

All of a sudden, they realize they've been spending all their time focused on the wrong things. They may have traded their passions for something seemingly more practical. They may have "inherited" their goals from their parents or society. They never stopped to truly consider what drives them—the "why" of what they do.

Entrepreneur: How does goal setting relate to rapid business *Pollard*: I once worked with a manufacturer in

Asia. This particular brand had an established presence and was one of the giants in the global market. However, it had gotten so big that it had become just another massive company. Innovative startups and smaller companies were eating away at its market share. The leadership team couldn't compete in the brand's respective product markets because they weren't agile enough.

After walking their hundred or so top execs through my rapid growth system, it became clear to themselves where they had been going wrong. They'd gone from being a company with a strong sense of purpose to one that tried to be all things to all people . . . resulting in them speaking to no one in particular. They had pursued growth by offering new features and products to new markets, yet continually lost market share.

They all went back to their respective divisions and teams with a clear way to communicate what the company wanted to achieve. That resulted in everyone being able to align their time, priorities, and activities. They went from rowing hard yet ineffectively to everybody pulling together: same boat, same rowers, same oars, but a vastly different speed.

Without that shared mission—or in the case of an individual business owner, that clarity of personal vision—it's easy to get distracted by every shiny object that comes along. You gravitate to tactics or the next big thing because you don't have a strong, internal sense of direction. You waste time chasing that edge because you've never sat down to ask yourself the important questions.

Entrepreneur: Figure out what you're even aiming for in the first place. What's after that?

Pollard: Once you have a clear idea of what you're doing, you need to clearly communicate it to the right people. Now, the modern approach to marketing says: one, find a niche willing to buy; two, create a marketing message for that market; three, create a sales system to sell to them.

If that's how you approach business, you're not harnessing all your potential energy or that of your team. You're trying to bind your company to a market that's not completely aligned with your identity. As a consequence, you and your team struggle to communicate what you do and often end up competing on price.

You have to first figure out what makes you tick or what gives your team a sense of purpose. There is a tremendous amount of energy that comes from being aligned with your why. Instead of employees leaving at five, you'll have to chase them out of the office.

Instead of being exhausted at the end of the day, I

often find myself energized and ready to do even more. That's what it looks like when you and your team have a clear vision that aligns with a deep sense of purpose.

Let me give you an example. I worked with the owner of a language tutoring company in California who faced increasingly difficult competition from translators undercutting her company's prices. She was even losing clients to people in China posting ads on Craigslist in L.A. offering the same services for pennies on the dollar.

We dug into her business and discovered a service that she provided for free: in teaching business executives Chinese to prepare for relocation to China. She also introduced them to some critical cultural concepts to help them succeed in business once they arrived there not because they asked her to, but because she truly loves to help people and wanted to see them succeed. Unsurprisingly, those executives, though few in number, were her best success stories and some of her biggest fans.

We created her unified message as the "China Success Coach" and her company as the "China Success Academy." She no longer competed against low-priced providers in her market. She was no longer a commodity to be compared against tutors on Craigslist. Her small company became a boutique provider of services for executives being relocated by their employers to China. Her unified message conveys everything in just three simple words.

For my part, I'm a business coach, a sales and marketing guy, a trainer, a social media guru—I'm so many things, yet nobody cares. If I were to begin an introduction or an advertisement with "business coach," plenty of people would be immediately turned off. They may have used a business coach before and feel like they wasted their money, so they tune out before I even finish speaking.

"The Rapid Growth Guy," on the other hand, unifies everything I do in just one phrase that doesn't mark me as a commodity as well as what intrigues the people I'm looking to work with.

When you tell someone you're the China Success Coach or the Rapid Growth Guy, instead of someone tuning you out, they often say, "What is that?" All of a sudden, you have their permission to talk about your products and services—instead of the usual approach of feeling like you have to shove your information down their throat.

This concept is even more powerful for larger corporations. Having a unified message isn't just for clients—it's a unifying message for your employees as well. Ideally, you want to create a unified message for each department or product line so that each niche you serve has its own purpose, and all are aligned with the greater unified corporate message.

Entrepreneur: I like that. In your approach, you create your own category. It separates you from the competition.

Pollard: Exactly. Customers can't compare you to others because you're no longer a commodity. No one else provides the products or services in quite the way you provide them. You go from being just another indistinguishable provider having to compete on price to becoming a category of one.

The clarity and simplicity of your message allows you to be overheard in a crowded marketplace where there are already hundreds or thousands of people all competing for the same customers.

Entrepreneur: It strikes me that this is somewhat similar to the aim of *Blue Ocean Strategy* where the authors show examples of companies who, instead of competing in the bloodbath of a feeding frenzy, created a whole new category of business and sailed out into the calm, clear waters of the wide-open ocean.

Pollard: That's right. They use Cirque du Soleil and Southwest Airlines as two good examples. We've had acrobats and clowns for generations. We've had airlines for a century. But while these companies' growth hack was to discover a blue ocean and then redefine their business around it, I suggest the opposite approach: discover your driving mission, then redefine your business around it. That, in turn, will lead you to discover your own market's blue ocean.

Most people, and especially small business owners, make the mistake of wanting to sell to everyone. You might let anyone buy from you, especially if it's a packaged product, but that's different than deciding on who you want to sell to.

The easiest approach to this exercise is to reflect on their past clients. Often, we have people we've sold to in the past who've bought from us with no problems, yet they don't sing our praises. On the other hand, we sometimes have people who sing our praises, but we don't make much money from them, if any.

What we're looking for are the people in the overlap: those who've made us money in the past and who also sing our praises. This is how we found the right market and message for the China Success Coach. Once we identified the people in the overlap, we explored what they had in common and why they were different from those other two groups.

Basically, you're discovering people who are as excited about your business as you are, who buy into your message, and who will become your biggest cheerleaders. By intentionally focusing on that kind of person, you're creating a whole tribe of people like them, instead of accidentally coming across one here or there as you attempt to sell to everybody.

Entrepreneur: And what do you do once you've crafted the right message?

Pollard: Then, you systemize your sales process. This is what my entire book *The Introvert's Edge* is about. Introverts like me don't have the gift of the gab like extroverts. The idea of selling usually terrifies us. Fortunately, that actually becomes a strength: instead of relying on our natural abilities, we have to rely on a process in order to successfully sell. After running my own sales teams and my own businesses, I've found that introverts make the best salespeople because they rely entirely on a process.

Once you turn sales into a system, you can then optimize that system just as you would a factory line. Henry Ford's genius wasn't the assembly line; it was his never-ending quest for efficiency. He constantly tinkered and changed his production lines to find ways to decrease the rate of defects here or how to shave 30 seconds off a process there. In modern business literature, many point to the example of Toyota for the same reasons and with the same results: consistently outperforming the competition by continually looking for ways to improve.

Sales is a process like any other. Hands down, those armed with a sales system will beat out those who aren't.

Entrepreneur: Then once you have your sales system in place?

Pollard: That's when you can start playing with tactics. That's when you see if hosting webinars drives more sales vs. offering a complimentary consultation, or how Facebook ads stack up against LinkedIn prospecting.

But those hacks' effectiveness will continually diminish if you don't have a solid foundation to begin with: your vision, your unified message, your ideal customer, and a systemized sales system. That's the key to true growth.

SUCCESSFULLY ORCHESTRATE THE EXPANSION OF A GROWING COMPANY

Marty Fukuda

To grow means to change, a thrilling yet daunting process for a business owner to witness at a company. If you're in a position of leadership, your team will look to you for explanations, solutions, and systems when things start to pick up and transitions take place.

Whether you anticipate steady growth or rapid expansion, follow these steps to circumvent common mistakes and maximize your firm's success.

1. Prepare Your Team

Working for a growing company is something your team should be proud of and excited by. Unfortunately, the opposite emotions can arise when an unexpected increase in new orders or clients catches staff off guard.

A good salesperson establishes realistic expectations for their customers. So why wouldn't you do the same for your employees? Whether your team consists of 3, 30, or 300 employees, gather them all together for a company-wide monthly update. I love using these types of meetings as an opportunity to talk about the future and what everyone can expect.

Your message should address the abundant opportunities that will accompany growth while not glossing over the challenges. Let members of the team know to anticipate some changes and bumps in the road and that everyone will need to contribute.

A team unprepared emotionally for the challenges of growth can be a huge distraction from an administrative standpoint. Keeping staffers informed about the strategic direction is a powerful deterrent to this type of roadblock.

2. Explain the Reasons for Expansion

For most entrepreneurially minded individuals, the reasons for growth are obvious. But this may not be the case for every member of your team. It's critical to inform members of your team about the inherent benefits of a company pursuing an upward trend.

Growing the business ultimately means more job security for the right people. Chances are you'll be adding team members to keep pace and certainly won't let go of a productive employee who's a good cultural fit. Be prepared that some may interpret this as a threat to their position. It's important to make sure your team understands your vision as well as how they fit into it. The more you can address their own personal fears, the more they'll be confident in their professional role. In talking about growth, emphasize the opportunities that growth will allow. Every growing organization needs leaders to spearhead the expansion, creating exhilarating opportunities for the right people. Promoting from within as much as possible will prompt engagement and higher performance from your team.

Another angle to talk about is risk. The larger your organization, the less vulnerable it will be to competitors or a single customer's departure. Paint a few scenarios about what you *don't* want to happen, like the cuts you'd have to make if you lost your number one customer tomorrow. Talk about the things you'd like to do but can't until you reach a certain size or revenue. Just because you spend your days and nights running through all the "what-if" scenarios doesn't mean your team does the same thing.

3. Don't Overthink Timing

Occasionally, I meet entrepreneurs shy about flipping the switch to pursue growth, fearing their company's systems are not ready for prime time. They want to ensure they've worked out every kink.

There's never a perfect time to strike. I'd rather err on the side of taking action today. If everything else is in place, there's nothing like an influx of new work to spur your team to improve.

Planning is necessary, but the ability to adapt is more important. Things will change that force you to change your plan. Instead of reacting to those inevitable changes, create a spirit of causing change. The more you pursue growth, the more prepared you'll be when you experience it.

4. Develop Scalable Systems

Even as you pursue growth, though, you need to focus on how your company will manage that growth. Start putting a plan in place now to make sure each department can scale up in size to meet the anticipated expansion. Take steps to prepare the team for the addition of new members, deciding who will train them and lead them, how work will be allocated, and what equipment or software should be purchased.

Make sure the tech you use is ready to handle the kind of volume you want. Check that you have a list of potential candidates ready for the different jobs you'll need to hire for so that you're not scrambling when growth hits. Talk to your vendors and suppliers to ensure that they can handle your growth.

Better yet, go read stories about all the companies that grew too fast and folded because they weren't prepared for it. They say the only thing worse than not enough customers is having too many. Make sure you're never in either boat.

5. Consider the Culture

Amid the chaos of rapid growth, it's easy to take your eye off the ball when it comes to culture. You shouldn't. Culture needs to be part of an ever-present initiative.

Think you have a great one now? See what happens if you double your team's size with no regard to the impact. I promise you, the culture will erode. My colleague at N2 Publishing, CEO Duane Hixon, is the first to say that defining the company's culture and educating new team members about expectations is a number-one priority—a task that has no finish.

Too many entrepreneurs forget about culture until it becomes a problem—and by then, it's so entrenched that the "fix" is more about damage control than positive reinforcement. As you grow, make sure you're growing in the right direction. Make sure you keep a clear vision of the kind of workplace environment you want, and make sure you communicate that vision. More importantly, listen to how your people talk about your culture.

Done right, culture can be your primary growth strategy.

6. Develop an Onboarding Strategy

This ties into the previous advice about culture, but it's important enough to be addressed individually: Have a process for bringing a new employee on board. Think back to the times you started a new job. What could they have done differently to help you plug into the company faster and ramp up your productivity faster? Ask your most recent hires about their onboarding experience: What could you have done better? What do they know now that they wish they'd known then?

7. Put a Leadership Team in Place

The larger an organization becomes, the more leaders you'll need. Identify people with the aptitude, attitude, and aspirations for leadership early in their careers so you can begin coaching them today for the roles you'll need filled tomorrow. Just like scaling your tech, operations, finance, and every other facet of the business, you need to scale your leadership.

WHY YOU SHOULD IGNORE THE SUCCESS OF FACEBOOK AND UBER

Per Bylund

Your chances of winning the Powerball grand prize are about 1 in 292 million. While that happy event is certainly not impossible, you probably wouldn't want to stake a business idea on those kinds of odds.

Those odds, by the way, are not that different from the probability of a college student's yearbook-themed website attracting more than 1 billion users and surging to a valuation of about $350 billion.

Still, the underlying challenge that Mark Zuckerberg and so many wannabes after him have faced hasn't stopped countless would-be entrepreneurs from attempting to recreate the meteoric success of the Facebooks and Ubers of the world. It's easy to see why with Facebook raking in about $9.1 billion in advertising revenue during the first three quarters of 2016 alone, according to a 2016 report in "The Information." That's more than media stalwarts such as CBS, Disney, and Comcast.

It's great to see young entrepreneurs inspired to seize success, but some of them are trying to replicate the magic of blockbuster companies that launched without working business models and instead offered a free service before miraculously pivoting to profitability with millions of users.

But maybe these young entrepreneurs should scale back their idealization of Facebook, Uber, and Snapchat because those companies are the exception—not the rule.

And they set a risky precedent. While traditional businesses in the past aimed for small-scale profitability before attempting to scale up, modern businesses seem designed solely to scale and to not turn a profit until they've reached some absurd threshold. And that means they can employ people for only a few months or years before having to close because they've run out of seed money and failed to reach unrealistic growth goals.

At that point, they'll disappear silently into the night.

But before that happens, they present eerie similarities to the dot-com boom and crash. People at the time talked about the dot-com bubble just like they do about these modern startups. They make fantastic promises but no profits.

The only difference is that today's situation is of much greater magnitude.

Making Money Without Charging a Thing?

Numerous young professionals have been led astray by the incredible success of companies such as Facebook, Snapchat, and Instagram. They see how seemingly simple it was for these ventures to build critical mass and cash in, neglecting the countless copycats who fell flat on their faces.

But entrepreneurs still determined to emulate Facebook by building critical mass and cashing in should check out an ongoing study started in 2014 by analytics firm CB Insights. Its researchers compile startup failure postmortem insights from founders and investors. An example? Political startup Poliana, which offered CB Insights the following nugget of wisdom: "The sad truth is that it's very hard to make money on something that deserves to be free."

Society largely considers the big-name internet companies to be successful when the truth is that few are actually making any money. Twitter, for one, has struggled to capitalize on its massive audience for years, according to a 2016 report by *Time*. Just because a company is well-known doesn't mean it has a sound business model.

So, rather than mimic these rare and highly publicized success stories, would-be entrepreneurs should focus instead on established practices and prudent entrepreneurship to build their businesses. Here are a few steps to get started.

1. Find a Market Before You Create Anything

Entrepreneurs sometimes get so excited about their idea that they create a product without considering customers. They might have mountains of market research, but it often focuses only on the size of their market and potential competitors.

When I lecture at Oklahoma State University, I stress the importance of finding a product-market fit. This fit can be determined only by first identifying what customers believe and how they behave. Entrepreneurs must offer them something they value on their own terms.

Will Caldwell, co-founder and CEO of mobile app developer Dizzle, is someone I mention in this context. Caldwell iterated several unsuccessful versions of the company's product before finally changing his approach.

When he finally focused less on offering "bells and whistles" and more on providing value to his market, things finally clicked. Customers were able to explain the product to him instead of the other way around, which helped him realize he had nailed his product-market fit.

2. Involve Customers in Product Development

When trying to determine a strong product-market fit, be sure to involve customers from day one.

By involving customers in product development, you can target your product to a customer persona with a proven interest, high problem awareness, and a willingness to pay. Illinois State University 2016 research shows that customer participation in new product development has a positive effect on innovation, speed to market, and financial performance.

So, when you choose a customer profile, make sure it offers profitability to your startup at a comparatively small volume. This will allow your business to scale by either expanding into other products for this same customer or by shifting the product to appeal to still other customers. Just don't try to do both at once.

I touch on this advice extensively in a course I teach on entrepreneurial thinking and behavior. I have my students conduct interviews with potential customers. And while they initially hate the experience, many say it becomes rather eye-opening over time. The students go through plenty of frustration during the learning process, and they often need to pivot in the face of empirical evidence contradicting their previous beliefs.

3. Be as Hands-on as Possible

Entrepreneurship is the opposite of secrecy and armchair philosophizing. To maximize your chances of profitability and impact, be hands-on with your product and customers to learn what they value. Nail down the problems they see and the solutions they might consider to help you develop and launch a profitable product.

The origin of Swiffer provides an illustrative example. As the story goes, Procter & Gamble leaders were looking for ways to increase the company's mop sales. As part of this research, they had design consultants visit with people in their homes to figure out ways to encourage customers to use mops more frequently.

During one of these meetings, a customer spilled coffee grounds on the floor. Instead of reaching for a mop, the elderly man picked up a damp paper towel to clean things up. When the consultants asked him why he didn't use a mop instead, he said the small pile of grounds wasn't worth the hassle of lugging out a mop and bucket.

This lone exchange served as the impetus for the concept of a "damp paper towel with a handle" . . . and the evolution of the standard mop.

Go Your Own Way

Gambling on a startup venture is always a risky proposition. According to a 2016 report from Startup Grind, some estimates suggest 90 percent end in failure. But the odds are definitely not in your favor if you try to mimic the rare rise of companies like Facebook or Uber.

Instead, employ the truly smart tactics likely to safeguard your startup. They include carefully studying your market; involving customers early in the process; and getting out of your office, incubator space, or garage to interact with your audience one-on-one.

8

HOW GROWTH HACKING IS REDEFINING MARKETING

Brett Relander

Over the years, marketing has been defined and redefined numerous times and in many different ways. At its core, however, marketing remains simply lead generation. Regardless of what you are marketing, or how you're marketing it, the goal is to drive awareness, demand, and sales. Unfortunately, many brands often miss opportunities because they forget that marketing is simply the vehicle used for getting customers.

Anything that can be used for driving awareness, creating demand, and accomplishing sales is marketing.

What Is Growth Hacking?

Recently, there has been much talk about growth hacking and whether it will or perhaps already has redefined marketing. If you're not already familiar with the concept, according to Aaron Ginn, a growth hacker is someone whose focus and passion pushes a metric-using methodology that is both scalable and testable. Ginn, a self-professed growth hacker, points out growth hackers will leverage multiple disciplines to extract insights and identify the right messages for pulling in users. The goal is to find a method that works and lead with it. This might prove to be traditional methods of marketing, but more often, it involves thinking out of the box and identifying innovative ideas for capturing a target audience's attention.

Andrew Chen, a writer, entrepreneur and tech startup advisor, recently referred to growth hacking as the "new VP of marketing." Pointing out that growth hacking has quickly become integrated into the culture of Silicon Valley, Chen emphasized that marketers must now possess a distinctive blend of both coding and marketing skills. No longer is marketing a single role. Instead, Chen claims that the lines between product development, engineering, and marketing are blurring, requiring everyone to work together. The key is integration and that requires a multitude of technical details.

Marketers are still focused on the best way to get customers interested in their products. What has shifted is how they are going about it. Rather than being people-centric, marketing has now made a transition to a technology-centric approach.

Just How Big Is Growth Hacking?

Tech Crunch reported in 2015 that AppVirality, an Indian startup that offers developers a dashboard for adding growth hacking techniques to their apps, has raised $465,000 in seed funding. By using the dashboard, developers can run A/B tests and view analytics to see the number of users they have reached through each specific tool. Additionally, the dashboard will allow developers to view the number of downloads as well as revenue their app has generated. With that much investment money injected, growth hacking is clearly on the rise.

While the new tool focuses on apps, growth hacking can be used on virtually anything, ranging from software to blogs to retail products. Hotmail is easily one of the best historical examples of early growth hacking in action when it launched way back in 1996. HootSuite reported in a 2015 article that by simply including the text "P.S. I love you" along with a link to their homepage on all emails sent using the Hotmail system, this brand was able to generate 12 million users in just one year.

Growth Hacking vs. Marketing

Growth marketing is not redefining the goal of marketing per se, but it certainly is changing the way that marketers go about the task of driving awareness, demand, and sales. Startup-Marketing. com points out in a 2014 article that the primary difference between growth marketing and traditional marketing is that growth marketers do not take the time to strategize a marketing plan. Instead, they test to find something that works.

You could think of growth hacking as the lean startup method for marketing. Instead of building a complex system or investing in expensive infrastructure, you quickly run with an idea to test its viability. When you find something that works, you scale it. Growth hacking works in much the same way. Traditional marketing often invested a lot of money in large scale projects: spending millions on a campaign ad or throwing money at digital marketing initiatives, for example. Growth hacking, instead, looks to find ways to drive demand, awareness, and sales by quickly pivoting and iterating. By the time something has gone mainstream so that many people feel safe about its reliability as a marketing tool, it's already lost much of its effectiveness.

Growth hackers, on the other hand, are leading from the bleeding edge.

IS GROWTH HACKING RIGHT FOR YOUR COMPANY?

Eric Siu

It's true: Growth hacking won't work for every company. But if you've already got a good product-market fit and a team that's on board with the idea of prioritizing growth through the adoption of new strategies and tactics, you're probably wondering how to get started with the strategy that's on everybody's lips these days.

Below, you'll find a simplified introduction to the process of growth hacking as many companies implement it. Pick and choose the pieces that work for your organization, and keep in mind that not every recommendation or step is appropriate for every company or industry.

Know Your Company—Inside and Out

Good growth hacking begins with an analysis of your company's strengths and weaknesses. Ideally, you've already determined that growth hacking is a good fit for you, but now you've got to dig deeper to figure out what specific challenges your organization is facing.

As an example, if you're the first to bring a product to market that offers your particular solution, one thing your growth hackers (or growth-hacking teams) will need to account for is the time required for consumer education. On the other hand, if you already have a rabid fan base of happy users, this strength gives you the unique leverage needed to consider deploying a referral bonus hack.

Next comes reexamining your company's systems to make sure that you can handle large-scale growth. All your processes and people need to be ready for the surge of customers and business you're aiming for.

Create Good Experiments

At their core, growth hackers rely on data to do their jobs.

Early in its formation, Dropbox—a great example of growth hacking—gave users a free gigabyte of online storage for bringing on new customers. Ultimately, the strategy was successful, as the company is now valued at $10 billion . . . but that doesn't mean this same approach will work for every growing company.

Imagine what would have happened if the additional costs associated with giving out free storage space would have made Dropbox unprofitable due to the need to build out its infrastructure? Or what if all those new users would have wound up unhappy with the service, abandoning Dropbox and telling others about their negative experiences along the way? Worse, imagine that Dropbox wouldn't have put any tracking or timeline features into place that would have allowed it to identify this failed experiment and change course in time.

Obviously, Dropbox's success makes such speculation seem irrelevant. But hopefully, you see the need to base any growth hacking initiatives around good experiments that include all of the following features:

- Measurements of the costs associated with launching a particular growth hack, as well as of the additional revenue generated by the program.
- Analytics tracking to measure the full impact of the hack (keep in mind that growth may occur in unexpected areas).
- Deadlines that allow growth hacking teams to assess the impact of a particular strategy and change course if necessary to avoid wasting resources on a program that's destined for failure.

Lather, rinse, and repeat. As long as you've set up your company's growth hacking experiments effectively, the key to success in this area lies in your organization's agility. Running a single test for a year, for example, might give you a wealth of interesting data but will ultimately limit your ability to make meaningful changes that result in positive growth.

Exercise Your Growth Hacking Muscles

Most companies doing growth hacking will approach these types of experiments in "sprints"—that is, quick periods of growth punctuated by evaluation periods. Depending on your company's product or service, these sprints could consist of a few days of experimentation followed by a day or two of wrap-up. If your sales cycle is longer, you may need a few weeks of experimentation to gather enough data to move forward.

Of course, it's also worth mentioning how important it is to make sure any growth you're driving through these sprints is sustainable for your organization. One particular experiment might drive your sign-up rates through the roof, but if you can't handle the influx of new business (whether due to lagging infrastructure or insufficient support resources), you're better off forgoing growth hacking entirely for a more scalable approach.

Just like any strenuous exercise, it's important to give your body time to recover. Don't be so focused on growth that you ignore the signs of fatigue, burnout, or worse. Look for flagging morale, missed deadlines, less innovation, and other such indicators to help you gauge how much sprinting your organization can handle.

Growth hacking isn't for everybody, so don't buy into the notion that hiring a rock star growth hacker will solve your company's lagging expansion once and for all. But if you're willing to adopt a mindset of growth as an organization and fully commit to each of the steps listed above, you may find that bringing growth hacking to your business gives you the tools and data needed to experience explosive growth.

10

GROWTH HACKING GONE WRONG

Raad Mobrem

The big new trend in the tech world and now in all industries is the cleverly coined term "growth hacking," which basically means the ability to quickly scale a product in creative ways outside of traditional marketing tactics. Think virality.

Companies like AirBnB, Dropbox, and Facebook are famous for it as they used specific hacks to grow their companies to a massive size.

For example, Dropbox, now valued at $10 billion, created a program that rewarded both the inviter and the invitee with one gigabyte of free online storage if the invitee signed up. This "hack" heavily contributed to the growth of Dropbox.

Despite the allure of a quick method that will lead to rapid scaling, growth hacking is not a fit for every company. The biggest misconception around growth hacking is that if your company puts some effort into it and tests different methods of "going viral," then your company will have the chance to become huge. This isn't always the case

How do I know this? As the co-founder of Lettuce, an online inventory and order-management system, I tried this strategy and made a few mistakes. Here are a few growth hacking misconceptions and how to overcome them.

1. Growth Hacking Can Happen at Any Stage

You can't grow a company that has an underdeveloped product or does not yet solve the problem of your target customer.

At Lettuce, we tried to force the growth of a solution that had not yet achieved product-market fit by developing a referral program too early in our company's life. We had seen a similar model work for other companies that growth hacked their way to success and thought that we could accomplish this as well. We chose to ignore the red flags.

At the time, our product was not yet great and we did not have a large enough customer base to even help drive the initial viral growth. However, we were so excited by the chance of incorporating a distribution hack into our system that we went ahead and implemented it. As a result, the entire referral program ended up yielding us zero customers and we wasted critical developer time.

Before you consider growth hacking, make sure you have achieved product-market fit.

2. A Growth Hacker Is the Solution.

Something every company needs to understand is that growth is not the job of a single "hacker" but should be the responsibility of the entire organization.

Initially, we made the mistake of hiring an employee whose sole role was to drive all of our growth. It ended up being a terrible situation for both sides. The creative hacks developed to drive leads did not yield sales and, thus, wasted time and money we could have spent on enhancing our product. We knew we needed to make changes.

We decided to put into place clearly defined goals our company was working towards: reducing the amount of leads lost, increasing revenue, and driving customer growth. To do this effectively, our marketing, sales, support, and product teams needed to come together to tackle these problems. We encouraged getting input from all departments to see which features—big or small—would help us reach our goals as quickly as possible.

Through learning from our mistakes, we no longer rely on the abilities and skills of a single person. Rather, we utilize and align the strengths of our entire team around common goals, focusing on first achieving product market fit and then growth.

3. Growth Hacking Can Work in Any Company

When we started brainstorming various hacks we could implement, we first looked at all the successful companies that experienced fast and sustainable growth through a viral-product mechanism. In doing this research, we realized each one of these products mimics everyday occurrences where communication is involved.

For instance, sellers on eBay would promote their store to their friends and network. Then those people realized that they could sell on eBay, too. This worked well because everyone sells (or wants to sell) various things at some point in their life. eBay was only mimicking this real-world occurrence with its tech platform, leading to incredible virality.

On the flip side, if we look at a company that sells complex airplane parts, it is unlikely they will have this type of virality.

What every company needs to understand is that the foundation of your solution needs to be able to tap into the power of a network to have growth hacking work in a substantial way. Working on growth mechanisms when the related foundation is not there will only bring small amounts of growth (at best).

Building these growth mechanisms is a long and hard journey but definitely not impossible. Just stay realistic about where your product is and whether you can tap into the network. Then figure out where you can drive growth in the funnel (starting from the bottom).

When you have achieved a comfortable conversion rate, or product-market fit, and your product can use the network, get creative and increase the top of the funnel with some clever hacks.

PART I
A CRASH COURSE ON GROWTH HACKING—REFLECTIONS

One thing everyone agrees on: growth hacking is a fundamentally different approach to marketing. It runs counter to conventional thinking, whether that's from strictly a marketing perspective or the broader business strategy.

As we said in the beginning of this section, the term is still new enough that we don't have a commonly agreed upon definition. That's why having so many perspectives—and especially divergent perspectives—is important.

The more points of view you consider . . . the more thoughtful ideas and real-word experience shared with you . . . the more you see what works and what doesn't . . . the more of a grasp you'll have on the concept.

The purpose of this section wasn't to put to rest the debate on what growth hacking is and whether it's a good thing or not. It was to present a survey of the field: Growth Hacking 101, if you will.

Now, get ready to dive even deeper.

GROWTH HACKS FOR YOUR MARKETING

I f Part I was a survey of the field, this is digging in deeper to some of the growth hacking in your marketing efforts. While these tend to be tech-heavy, we wanted to balance out the perspective by including a rather unique growth hack expert interview: the founder of UGG Boots.

Just the reference of "growth hacking marketing" brings to mind social media and other digital tools. While those have their place, don't limit yourself to online growth hacking. UGG's success growth came primarily from guerilla marketing efforts but, more importantly, from the entrepreneur's confidence in himself, his business, and his inevitable success—aspects of the entrepreneurial spirit that transcend time and tech.

If the authors had one wish to grant you around growth hacks for your marketing, it wouldn't be to teach you how to use a specific tool. Rather, it would be to convince you to embrace the idea that, to find successful growth hacks, you have to be prepared to look at your business—and even the world—differently than most people do. They would want you to see what others can't see—to think about your marketing completely different than others.

As Proust said, "The real voyage of discovery consists not in seeking new landscapes, but in having new eyes."

11

GROWTH HACK STRATEGIES ANY BUSINESS CAN USE

Sujan Patel

So let's say you launched a business and it's starting to grow, but you desperately want to expand your audience and customer base. To achieve this goal, you need to execute a forward-thinking marketing strategy.

Growing a business isn't easy because there are so many bases to cover, from reducing churn, to delighting customers, to content marketing, to new customer acquisition.

There are also plenty of ways to lose business en route. Thankfully, with some simple tactics and a solid strategy, you can gain traction while your competitors are still struggling.

Here are the top eight growth hack ideas that any business can implement to bolster its efforts.

1. Get Active at the Right Time

Have you ever noticed that musical artists tend to release tracks toward the beginning of the week? That's when you're most likely to capture people's attention. With this in mind, it might be a good idea to time your content publishing schedule and marketing campaigns to roll out on Tuesdays or Wednesdays.

This advice isn't universal, however. Your particular audience might display different behavior, so do some research beforehand to find out when they're most active online. That will give you insight into the best times for media releases, social posts, ads, and other promotions, according to Buffer.

2. Keep Your Opt-In Visible

If you want to keep your audience's attention, put your opt-in near the top of your pages. If you don't want a static opt-in, then test the effectiveness of drop-in or slide-in opt-ins. Make sure your site is also optimized for mobile users and can easily avoid penalties from any of Google's updates.

"Don't make people dig around your site to stumble across subscription options," writes Andy Pitre, inbound marketer for HubSpot. "Keep your offers up-front and include calls-to-action on just about every page of your website."

This can also be used to sway exit-intent behaviors.

3. Embed Social Content

Social proof is a great way to build trust. Rather than pasting generic-sounding testimonials, go find social mentions for your brand. Embed tweets or content from other social channels directly onto your site. Social reviews will always be perceived as more trustworthy when they can be easily traced back to the original source.

4. Claim Broken Links

This is one of my favorite methods for building a natural link profile and gaining referral traffic. Find high-quality resource lists that mention brands, products, topics, or services similar to your own.

Search through the lists for broken links with a simple tool, and reach out to the publisher if you find a broken link. Offer your resource as an alternative to keep the link alive rather than deleting it.

Another approach is to scout around for broken links on high-value sites, and then build content specifically designed to replace the link before you contact them. This lets you customize the content to fit that site and its audience.

"Creating content that is a perfect substitute for a broken page will obviously take more time," writes Neil Patel, founder of Quicksprout. "But it will get you a higher conversion rate."

5. Connect with Influencers

Every industry has people who wield massive influence over a target audience. Consumers trust their insight and experience. Connect with those influencers and offer discounts or free access/products in exchange for some promotion.

If they're not interested in that exchange, find out if they do sponsored shoutouts and determine the costs involved. This is usually an affordable way to get your product mentioned in front of a large audience.

6. Improve the New User Experience

New customers have different needs from those of recurring customers. When you acquire a completely new customer, they are initially going to be highly critical of everything you do. New customers have certain expectations that need to be met before they feel comfortable.

You can win them over and increase the likelihood of better referrals by creating a better onboarding process.

Once the new customer makes that first purchase, provide supportive content that will continue the conversation and education beyond the initial handshake. This will help you build a relationship and let the customer know that you value him or her beyond the first transaction.

7. Build Your Authority

I'm always impressed when I see influencers and figureheads for major brands spending their time in discussion groups and on sites like Quora. It says a lot when someone is willing to take time out of a busy day to provide free advice and information for others.

This is a great way to build visibility for your brand. You'll find topics, questions, and discussions that are relevant to just about every industry if you browse a little while. Provide insight for free and you'll develop a group of followers who might later transform into brand advocates for your business.

8. Get It Done Now

You can't base your entire strategy on long-term goals; you also need to spend time scoring quick wins. Figure out which things aren't exactly scalable but will get customers buying from you right now. Those quick wins may only be short-term solutions, but they'll immediately generate revenue that you can use for future growth.

"Startups take off because the founders make them take off," writes Paul Graham of Y Combinator. "There may be a handful that just grew by themselves, but usually it takes some sort of push to get them going. A good metaphor would be the cranks that car engines had before they got electric starters. Once the engine was going, it would keep going, but there was a separate and laborious process to get it going."

Get some great momentum with growth hacks, and then build on that momentum to keep it up.

FIVE GROWTH HACKING SECRETS FOR YOUR SAAS BUSINESS

Thomas Smale

Building a business from the ground up can be a long road. You've spent a lot of time coming up with a unique SaaS idea that cold-generates value for your target audience, and now you just want to see that business grow.

SaaS describes a software-licensing and delivery model where cloud-based software is licensed via subscription and is centrally hosted. And this may be your business model. If so, the prospect of using that model to become a ten-years-in-the-making "overnight" success may strike you as distinctly unappealing.

That will mean you'll have to find a way to hack your way to growth. Here are five growth hacking secrets for your SaaS business.

1. Give Away Something Valuable

To convince people to use your service, consider giving something away. A 30-day trial is commonplace and not much of an incentive. Likewise, an iPad giveaway might be a way to drive some initial interest, but is too generic an offer to be valuable—particularly if it isn't connected to your service in some way.

But there are other useful ideas out there. When Dropbox first started, it gave away a lot of extra storage through its referral program. Whenever you sent a friend or colleague an invite to join and they followed through, Dropbox granted you even more storage.

This turned out to be a great strategy for the company whose product was virtual storage space in the cloud. Its customers helped spread the word about the service, and pretty soon, Dropbox grew like crazy. Incidentally, PayPal did something similar: It initially awarded $10 for each referral. Who wouldn't want a bit of extra cash? Paypal saw huge growth as result of this promotion.

How can you get your own customers involved? What can you do to get people to market your business for you? Follow the lead of Dropbox and PayPal: Consider giving away something that connects directly to what your business offers. Share the fruits of your labor without giving away the entire farm.

2. Leverage the Freemium Model

People love free stuff, and offering your service for free can be a great way to get some early traction.

Is your value proposition hard to understand? Is it a sophisticated software service that requires user education? Is it complex or just hard to explain in other ways? You need potential users to see the value in what you offer. In a situation like that, the freemium business model can really work. Evernote, for instance, experienced a lot of challenges in the early stages of its business. But, by offering its software for free, it was able to grow its user base and help people understand the value of its offering.

Today, you can still sign up to Evernote for free, but the company has pricing plans for power users as well.

3. Create Compelling Content

If you want to build your business with content, you have to be sold on the idea 100 percent. You can't dip your toe into the water and expect to see results. You must commit to publishing content that is steady, regular, and—most of all—high quality.

Content, however, can be a great differentiator in a crowded market. Some experts even say it's the only way to differentiate yourself from other businesses. When Buffer first made an entrance into the social media tool niche, it was just one among many. But by creating incredibly valuable content and sharing it on social media, it was able to attract a huge audience over time.

Content often goes hand in hand with building an email list. Having a large database can easily translate into more traffic and more money. Noah Kagan of AppSumo was able to build an email list of over 700,000 members by leveraging a variety of different tactics, many of which were connected to content. This allowed him to get his service out to a huge buying audience.

Building an audience and an email list takes time. But once you've done the work, you'll have built a loyal following that will take interest in whatever software you release.

4. Make Partners From Your Competition

Odds are that you've already done a competitive analysis, so you know whom you're up against in your market. You've thought about what your differentiating factors are and how you're going to innovate and stand out from the crowd.

What you may not know about is the potential opportunity to leverage the popular platforms others have created. Is there a giant in your industry that has a majority of the market share? If so, becoming a direct competitor could be the path of greatest resistance. But if you can make a partner out of that business, you can hack your way to big growth that way.

This is exactly what Airbnb did when it recognized the ubiquity Craigslist had. Craigslist was already dominant in the rentals, temporary residence, and vacation-home market when Airbnb started looking to grow its own user base.

Instead of investing increasing amounts of money into advertising, Airbnb did something smart; it asked users to add their personal listings to Craigslist as well. This wasn't exactly easy since Craigslist did not have an API (meaning an application program interface whose protocols and tools help build a new software application), but Airbnb managed to figure things out with a bit of coding wizardry.

5. Make Your Offering Exclusive

Exclusivity stands as a prominent strategy for growing a SaaS business. For one thing, it allows you to scale your business without feeling a huge amount of pressure. Another important component to this strategy is that, psychologically, people want to be a part of the "in crowd"—not left out.

LinkedIn achieved this exclusivity by making its social network about professionals. And Google did it with Gmail: you had to get an invitation to get your personal inbox.

Social media scheduling tool MeetEdgar is another great example of an "exclusive" software. If you go to MeetEdgar's homepage, you'll see that the only thing it lets you do is enter your email address to request an invitation.

So, do the same. Appeal to the "cool kids" by creating a compelling reason for people to sign up; then, get them to share your service with their friends.

Final Thoughts

Another way to hack your way to profit is to buy a SaaS business. Even if you know your way around only a couple of niches, you can often find a business well-matched to your skills. Growth hacking may provide opportunities for quick growth, but that doesn't mean there isn't any work involved. As with the example of content marketing, a concerted and dedicated effort is often necessary to pull off a growth strategy.

FIVE GROWTH HACKS FOR APP DOWNLOADS

Steve Young

According to mobile marketing technology firm Fisku, cost per install in November of 2015 for iOS increased 40 percent from $1.10 to $1.54, while Android increased an astonishing 101 percent from $1.13 to $2.27 year-over-year.

With the cost per install consistently growing each year, app publishers must get creative with their marketing efforts. After successfully launching apps of our own and also for our clients, you will discover five of our favorite growth hacks to increase downloads when you have little to no budget.

1. Paid-to-Free Campaign

This is a campaign that I have run many times, and it's driven hundreds of thousands of downloads on multiple occasions. If you're not familiar with a paid-to-free campaign, it's where you make a paid app available for free for a couple of days.

If you have a free app, you can make one of your in-app purchases free. However, the in-app purchase must be a non-consumable type, which means that the product is purchased once by users and does not expire or decrease with use. For example, new race tracks for a game could be implemented as non-consumable products.

It is important to note that getting media exposure is crucial to making this a successful campaign. I generally give a big website like AppAdvice or BGR the exclusive on the free campaign, which dramatically increases the chances that the website will cover the price change. Skip to the fourth strategy of this chapter to learn more about the exclusive strategy.

2. App Store Optimization

There are two commonly overlooked components of your app store listing page that can increase your downloads: reviews and in-app purchases.

The words that are in your app store reviews—those left by your users—and in-app purchases are all indexed by Google Play and iOS. Having targeted, relevant keywords in both areas will help you see a dramatic increase in downloads.

3. Localization

There are 28 regions in the App Store, and each country has its own App Store. It would be naïve to think that the world only searches for apps in English. In fact, most users will read and search the App Store in their native language. Unless your app is designed for a specific region, take the time to localize your app in every language. You never know who will find your app useful.

Gonzalo Juarez, co-founder at eTips, the number-one publisher of mobile travel apps, proudly admits that they do not run any paid marketing campaigns. Localizing his apps has led to a greater than 200 percent increase in downloads and in countries where they didn't have exposure before.

Juarez suggests first translating the words used in your app name and keyword field. Once you start to notice an increase in downloads for a particular language, he suggests further translating your app description, screenshots, and then finally your in-app content.

Lastly, use a translation website like Gengo or OneHourTranslation and hire two translators: one to do the initial translation and another to proof it.

4. Leverage PR

Using the exclusive strategy, we have been able to secure coverage on Techcrunch, Social Times, AppAdvicek, and BGR.

What is it? You give a big publication the first right to publish your announcement: product release, update, funding, etc. Big sites love getting an exclusive because it means that they will be the first to write about the announcement, which generally leads to the other big websites linking back to them as the source.

It's a win-win strategy because they get traffic and backlinks while you get coverage.

The key to success for this strategy is to start early. You want to start pitching about two weeks before your launch date. You should only pitch the exclusive to one publication at a time and be sure to follow up only once. If you do not hear back, you can move on to the next publication.

5. App Store Hack

There's a little-known strategy that I've used to help multiple clients get featured by Apple. Before we get to that, it's important to know what Apple is looking for in your app.

Most developers know that they can email appstorepromotion@apple.com to pitch their apps for a possible feature. However, within Apple, there are "app store managers" for each app category.

Using a LinkedIn search for "app store manager," you can find out how to contact the right person to pitch at Apple. I like to use the Chrome extension Email Hunter because it automatically creates an "email" button within LinkedIn that reveals the person's email address. The software makes an educated guess of the email, so sometimes you may get a bounce back.

Growth hack opportunities change all the time, though. Just by writing this, my App Store hack will lose some of its effectiveness as more people learn about it. That's why the idea of growth hacking is more important than any one hack: You have to constantly be looking for the next new thing and get ahead of the curve.

ENTREPRENEUR VOICES SPOTLIGHT: INTERVIEW WITH BRIAN SMITH

Founder of UGG Boots

Someone once quoted Eddie Cantor as saying, "It takes 20 years to make an overnight success."

That's the story of UGG Boots in a nutshell. One day, Brian Smith was peddling these weird Australian sheepskin boots out of the trunk of his car. The next day, it seemed every celebrity in the world sported a pair.

How did he pull it off?

Entrepreneur: Brian, you talk about your 17-year journey at the helm of UGG in your book *The Birth of a Brand*. One of your key ideas is that you can't just start a billion-dollar business.

Smith: That's right. There's a process. It's just like having a child. You can't give birth to an adult. You have to conceive it first. Then you give birth to an infant. In infancy, a baby doesn't do much. You have to continually feed it, change its diapers, and worry about whether you're doing everything right or not. Every business has its infancy where it seems like nothing is really happening and you see no traction. That's why so many entrepreneurs give up in the early days. They think because they're not seeing any success, they must not be doing the right thing.

But if you can get through the infancy stage, your business will start toddling. It may not be able to stand up on its own, but you start to see the potential of what's to come. It starts gaining some independence, but it has to get some bumps and bruises along the way.

Then comes the youth phase. This is the really cool part of the business. Things are happening, people are taking notice, and you have something that you're quite proud of. It looks healthy, it's developing, and it's a joy to watch it grow.

Then come the teenage years. Every teenager wants to go to every party in town—to be seen as the cool kid who's everywhere doing everything. You start seeing that there are much bigger games out there where the stakes are much higher. Just like raising a teenager, this is a dangerous stage for a business. Making the wrong decisions, running with the wrong crowd, and listening to the wrong people can have lasting consequences. In addition to all that, there are also the internal changes—those awkward years when a teenager is caught between being a child and an adult physically, mentally, and emotionally. I almost lost UGG a few times during this phase. You need guidance, mentors, and rules to survive.

But if you can survive the teenage years, you'll soon find that you've raised a mature, self-reliant adult. And if you've done a really good job, it's something that becomes more than you ever imagined.

Entrepreneur: And your advice to entrepreneurs looking for growth is to realize that every business has to go through these stages?

Smith: Absolutely. Again, you can't give birth to an adult. Now, with technology, you may be able to accelerate these stages—your business may mature faster than your competitors'—but you can't skip infancy and go to being a mature adult. You have to crawl before you can run.

Entrepreneur: Continuing your analogy, can you talk about some of the times UGG experienced growth spurts?

Smith: Yes, keeping in mind that these were growth spurts appropriate to the stage the business was in at the time. In my first year—UGG's infancy—I sold 28 pairs: exactly a thousand dollars. Over the next couple of years, I only sold a few hundred pairs. I couldn't break into any of the wholesalers, much less serious retailers.

I was having a beer with a guy at a surf shop talking about my problems and he said, "Shut up, Brian. Hey, guys!"—there were some young surfer kids out back—"Come over here. Hey, me and my friend here are talking about those UGG boots. Have you seen those? What do you guys think about them?"

They said, "Oh, man, those guys are so fake! Have you seen their ads? Those models can't surf. So fake."

I ran magazine ads of beautiful models wearing UGG boots on the beach; I thought that was the way you advertised. Once I realized I was sending the wrong message to my target market, I quickly pivoted. By then, I didn't have much money for marketing, but I had to come up with something. I found a couple of young surfers who were on the cusp of turning pro. I took my own camera and just went surfing with them at Black's Beach and Trestles. The walk to each is about a mile and it's a fantastic surf at the end. I knew that every kid reading the magazine would die to be on that walk with Mike Parsons or Ted Robinson. I found a way to put some passion into the ad so that it connected emotionally with the reader.

Sales jumped from $20,000 to $200,000.

Entrepreneur: Because of the right ad.

Smith: Because of the right *connection*.

I had confidence in sheepskin boots. Everyone who ever tried a pair on instantly loved them. They're amazing. I had confidence in my product. I also had confidence in my market: active sports enthusiasts who wanted footwear that worked with whatever they were doing. The challenge was finding the emotional connection between my product and my market.

For instance, when we got ready to expand into the Midwest, they don't buy like California. I couldn't use surfers or young skiers because that's not the Midwest. So I said, "What the hell do kids in Minnesota do?"

Well, all the kids are in hockey leagues. They all had to change shoes before they went out on the ice, and with them were their mothers sitting in these skating rinks in the freezing cold watching their kids. We started advertising to the young hockey market, and the same thing happened: we went from sales of almost nothing to hundreds of thousands of dollars overnight . . . because we found the right connection.

Entrepreneur: Wow, talk about ten times the growth. What's another time UGG experienced something similar?

Smith: I was on a plane coming home to San Diego, sitting next to a girl reading *People* magazine. Every page was a picture of some celebrity in their everyday clothes going around town. Of course, by doing so, they were indirectly advertising for Gucci or Prada or whoever.

I wondered, *How could I get into that?*

I did some digging and found out about Hollywood stylists—the makeup and wardrobe people working with all these actors. I found a mailing list for about 400 of them. I sent a letter to each of them asking if they'd like a free pair of UGG boots and if so to give me a call. About 40 stylists responded, and we sent each of them a pair of boots.

Over the next two years, UGG boots started showing up on the Hollywood scene. Tabloids might photograph someone relaxing on set in-between scenes and they happen to have a pair of UGGs on. Brooke Shields had a pair on in a sitcom. Then there was a movie scene where Tom Cruise has his feet propped up on a table in a pair. You couldn't buy that kind of advertising!

Once that momentum started, everybody in Hollywood wanted a pair of UGGs. They were everywhere. All the retailers in Los Angeles were scrambling to place orders. Sales soared—all from giving free boots to 40 stylists.

Entrepreneur: That is guerilla marketing at its finest. Send us off with a third and final growth spurt.

Smith: When I think about this next example, I want to start by saying something I've learned—and one of the things I try to convey in my book—is that, as an entrepreneur, your worst disappointments often become your greatest blessings. When things don't turn out like you thought they would, it makes you think about a new way of doing something. Often, after running up against a brick wall and getting a bloody nose, I'd have to step back for a day or two and try to figure out how to get around it. The situation would force me to look at it differently, and I'd go, "Oh my god—why didn't I think of that earlier!" And I'd find an even better way of going about it.

Here's the story. Once we had gotten into a lot of niche markets, I wanted to find a way to project a national brand—a way of bringing all these different segments together. I came up with the theme of casual comfort. I knew that if we really wanted to go national, we needed to be featured in a national publication, so I set my sights on the front cover of *USA Today*'s lifestyle section.

I hired a public relations agency for $65,000. We put together a huge presentation and landed an appointment with the fashion editor for the newspaper. We got to her office in Chicago and got set up for my big presentation. She came in apologizing, saying she was double-booked. She had a conference call at three o'clock; she could give us five minutes.

All I had time for was to quickly leaf through a tattered old file where I kept all the clippings of celebrities and athletes wearing UGG boots. She asked a couple of questions, asked for our press kit, and thanked us for our time. The whole meeting lasted maybe four minutes.

I just sat there looking at the PR woman with me. "We just totally blew it, didn't we? Sixty-five thousand dollars and all that time down the drain."

The next morning, I was in O'Hare preparing to fly back to San Diego. I picked up a *USA Today* with my coffee and on the cover of the lifestyle section was a picture of Pamela Anderson on the set for *Buywatch* wearing a pair of tall UGG boots!

But then I went from thrilled to pissed off once I read the article. The editor had written the piece on the topic of shearling (sheepskin) footwear, from its history to major manufacturers. Instead of an article on UGG, we were listed alongside all our competitors!

I didn't realize it right then, but she did me a huge favor: she legitimized a category. Whereas before, Nordstrom's and Saks Fifth Avenue had shut me out. Now they saw UGG not as a product, but as the leader of a footwear category. Her article made it safe for these retailers to carry our product. When I landed in San Diego, they told me that our phones had been ringing off the hook. Everybody wanted to know who in their area carried UGG boots.

The lesson for me there was twofold. First, I learned to reframe how I presented a new idea in terms of something familiar; I learned how to make it easy for people to wrap their head around something new and different.

The other lesson is that there is always an opportunity in the obstacle. But you have to be willing to look past the disappointment to find it.

SIX GROWTH HACKING TIPS FOR CONTENT MARKETERS

Abdullahi Muhammed

Want to stand out online? To truly get noticed in the increasingly crowded world that is the internet, you need to learn how to market your content in new and creative ways.

A Facebook post here or there and an occasional email campaign will no longer cut it. You have to be willing to use every method at your disposal to get your content in front of new eyes and grow your audience.

Luckily, there are a few simple hacks that will allow you to explode the success of your content marketing campaigns and put your business on the fast track to success.

1. Publish High-Performing Content

The first and most important step in any content marketing campaign is creating high quality content that your audience needs and wants.

Without the high quality content to back up your marketing efforts, you will never be able to truly succeed. The real struggle that most entrepreneurs face, however, is not actually creating great content. It is finding the content to create in the first place.

Luckily, Buzzsumo has a free tool that allows you to analyze trending content and discover the highest performing topics within your niche.

With a few simple searches, you can create a list of hot topics that will exponentially increase the success of your content marketing campaigns.

2. Start Blogging on LinkedIn

As far as social media goes, LinkedIn is an efficient way to grow your network, your brand, and your authority at a rapid pace.

One of the best ways to take advantage of LinkedIn is to start publishing blog posts directly onto its Pulse platform.

While it will probably not generate the same level of traffic you might expect from other content marketing methods, the professionalism of LinkedIn will help you increase your authority within your niche and position yourself as an expert in your field.

3. Gamify Your Blog

With the recent rage of online and social media gaming, the power of gamification is clearer now more than ever before.

A great way to build your audience, improve the shareability of your content, and increase user engagement on your blog is to gamify your blog with things like badges, votes, and personalized user accounts.

There are a number of WordPress plugins that you can use to help gamify your blog, and while this may not be a direct method of marketing your content, in the long run, it's a great marketing hack to have a product or service that people love using.

By gamifying your blog, you will have people coming back to you on a more regular basis and enjoying your content a hell of a lot more.

4. Think Outside the Box

If you are an online entrepreneur who relies solely on your blog for generating content, then you need to think outside of the box and step outside of your comfort zone.

Start creating YouTube videos, podcasts, Udemy courses, and slideshow presentations.

Not only will you have more success in your content marketing efforts by using a wider variety of platforms, but you will also open up the doors for potential revenue streams you had never considered before.

5. Write More

If you want your content to rank on the first page of Google for any keyword—and I am assuming you do—then you need to start writing more.

I see a lot of bloggers who focus on quantity over quality, publishing a dozen or so 500 word articles each month, never realizing that the true way to rise through the ranks of Google and effectively market your content is to write fewer articles that are longer and offer more value.

6. Post Content on Social Media More Than Once

Lots of bloggers believe that they can only share new content on social media once.

The simple truth, however, is that if you want to have success in online entrepreneurship, then you need to start sharing your content several times across several platforms. There are even tools to help you automate this.

While you will typically generate the most clicks on the first day that you share new content, you will have more views, likes, and shares if you are sharing your content more than once.

I recommend sharing new content three times over the course of the first week of its publication. In my experience, you will typically have a reduction in your click rate of about 20 to 30 percent for each additional day that you post.

But if you do the math, sharing an article three times that has 100 views on the first day with a 20 percent reduction in click-throughs would still generate an extra 96 views in the first week!

Conclusion

The internet is crowded with new content on a daily basis, and standing out from this crowd is no easy task.

However, if you are willing to take an unconventional approach to content marketing, you can start to generate more traffic to your content than ever before. By thinking outside of the box and utilizing tactics that most entrepreneurs do not even know about, you will quickly propel your content (and your revenue) to new levels.

15

SIX GROWTH HACK TECHNIQUES YOU CAN TRY TODAY

Neil Patel

Growth hacking has changed the game for today's marketers. However, a lot of people are confused as to what growth hacking actually is. Sure, it's different from traditional marketing, but *how* and *why*? And what does it all mean?

One of the best ways to understand growth hacking is to *do* growth hacking. Not only will you begin to understand how it works, but you'll also experience its growth potential.

Here are six growth hacking techniques you can implement in your own company:

1. Start a Blog

"Wait, give me some real techniques," you're thinking.

Actually, I'm serious about this. A blog is an essential tool in the growth hacker's toolbox.

But don't let the word "blog" throw you off. What I'm aiming at is a full-fledged content marketing effort.

Growth hacking runs on the engine of content. You've heard it so many times it makes you nauseous: "Content is king."

It's true. Whatever method you choose—blogging, Instagram, Slideshare, infographics—content matters.

The better you become at creating content, promoting content, and sustaining an output of content, the better you'll be at growth hacking. Today's customers—yep, even your customers—want content. They read content and they convert based on content.

Growth hacking means content marketing.

2. Guest Post

As marketers should know by now, traditional "link building" is history. Gone are the days when you could rustle up a few link-backs after sending some emails and pulling a few strings.

How do you grow your brand today and get those coveted link-backs?

It's called guest posting. Even though it irks the powers that be, it still works. As long as you're creating high-quality content on high-quality sites, you'll get the high-quality growth that you deserve.

Here's how you do it: Identify the leading websites in your niche, and pitch them with a request to provide an article.

3. Build Your Personal Brand

Growth hacking is enhanced by personal branding.

Today's top growth hackers are well-known people like Elon Musk, Richard Branson, Tim Ferriss, and Jeff Bezos. These entrepreneurs didn't approach growth like a typical CMO. They hacked their way in, creating massive disruptions as they did so.

If you can become a small-time celebrity in your own right, then you're already positioned to start killing it with growth hacking.

One does not simply "become a small-time celebrity" without a lot of hard work and hustle. It's not easy to become well known, but neither is it impossible in the age of digital marketing. With a computer and a connection, you have the basic building blocks of a personal brand.

As you build your own brand, you can build other brands, too. That's what we call growth hacking.

How do you do it? Spend time intentionally curating your own social profiles and personally engaging online. It takes time, but you'll get there eventually.

4. Harvest Email Addressed

The rage over social media is overrated.

Email remains the king of lead gen, with three times as many active users than all the social media users combined, according to Kissmetrics. It's 40 times more effective than Facebook and Twitter. Email marketing has three times the purchase potential of social media, and pulls in average orders that are 17 percent higher. Even though it's one of the oldest digital marketing channels, it's still the best. And it's still growing.

This is a growth hacking channel too big to ignore.

Growth hackers may speak softly, but they carry a big email list. If your goal is to hack some growth, then you need to grow your email list.

There's a quick and dirty way to do this. Simply create an email opt-in form on your website.

Or, you can use a popup for maximum email harvesting.

5. Hire a Growth Hacker

Growth hacking has become this big, bloated, misunderstood field. Hire a growth hacker.

Before you go Craigslist-happy with a job ad, do a reality check. Growth hackers don't grow on trees. Growth hackers have become as common as the self-proclaimed "social media gurus" littering the Twitter landscape. People like to use the word "growth hacker" in their LinkedIn title because it sounds trendy and they attended a webinar on it.

Be careful when selecting, vetting, and hiring a growth hacker. Do your homework on growth hacking so you can hire a good one.

6. Really Understand Your Data

Just because growth hacking has the word "hack" in it doesn't mean that it's sloppy or haphazard. Growth hacking is obsessively focused on data.

Data leads the way in the growth hacking environment. It's crucial that you understand key performance indicators (KPIs), viral coefficients, multivariate testing, CACs, LTVs, and other jargon-y metrics.

More analytics companies are streamlining and presenting data in ways that feed the growth hacking engine. When you start to really understand your data, you'll be better equipped to launch growth hacking.

Data doesn't always mean numbers. Data is *information.* You need content performance information (Buzzumo), customer acquisition data (Colibri.io), customer information (Kissmetrics), and other actionable information. Don't rely on something like Google Analytics for all your data needs. Dig a little deeper by using an analytics platform that interprets your data in actionable ways.

Growth hacking isn't any easier than traditional growth methods . . . but it is more effective.

SEVEN THINGS TO OUTSOURCE IMMEDIATELY TO SCALE YOUR BUSINESS

Sujan Patel

The hallmark of any entrepreneur is the ability to wear multiple hats, juggle dozens of tasks simultaneously, and multitask their way from startup to consistent income stream.

Ironically, though, multitasking can actually damage your brain and decrease your productivity. Studies are rife with statistics and case studies showing that the human brain lacks the capacity to successfully perform more than one task at one time.

So what's the solution? Option one is to grow your business slowly and give yourself the time to exclusively manage single tasks. However, if you're like me, you love building and running your business and don't want to scale at such a painfully slow pace.

The other solution is to immediately outsource specialized and tedious tasks to free up your time while you simultaneously scale your business.

Here are seven ways to get started on option two.

1. Conversion Optimization

According to HubSpot writer Lindsay Kolowich, approximately 96 percent of people who visit your website aren't ready to buy from you. That means you either need to optimize your conversions for greater sales and profit or be content with living off that 4 percent of customers you're actually selling to.

The good news is that it's possible to give your conversions a dramatic boost through content marketing, product reviews, improvements to your sales funnel, and guest-speaker opportunities.

But, do you know which one will work best for your company and how they might all work together? Instead of wasting time and money on guessing and experimenting, outsource to an outside expert the conversion strategies you need. The sooner you improve those conversions, the faster you'll profit and scale your way to success.

2. Customer Support

It can take entrepreneurs years to hone their messaging and create a steady stream of sales. But it can take just a few minutes to lose a customer's loyalty with poor customer service. Hire a virtual assistant skilled in your industry and the products and services you offer. Comb through LinkedIn and look for recommendations through your network, or utilize LinkedIn groups to find someone who aligns with your needs.

Customer service pros can help you focus on the channels your customers use the most. For example, Live Chat support can help you resolve issues the moment a customer comes to your site to look for your contact information—or help you close a sale by answering questions about your product or service.

3. Lead Generation

If lead generation were easy, we wouldn't constantly read articles about entrepreneurs failing 90 percent of the time. Like conversion optimization, lead generation is difficult and directly impacts how far you can scale your business. It's also incredibly time consuming and technical and can take more time and skill than you have in your business arsenal.

It's possible you can handle lead generation in-house and save on the cost of a lead agency. But you still need to consider the trickle-down costs involved. Outsourcing lead generation can save you a bundle on hiring sales teams to make cold calls, run ads, and figure out the optimal marketing strategy.

4. Automate Income Streams

Juggling too many projects and clients distracts from creating income streams that help keep your business running. You can't possibly be a business coach, investor, digital product creator, and public speaker without losing focus and letting the important details slip through the cracks.

However, you can hire a virtual assistant to do just about anything you would ordinarily do. Hire someone to track down research and pull together data on projects you want to pursue. Then, hire someone else to keep it all running. For example, an entrepreneur interested in real estate can get started on Realty Mogul for as little as $5,000. A virtual assistant skilled in real estate can help keep track of potential deals and your investments.

Meanwhile, an entrepreneur who wants to create a course on growth hacking could hire someone to set up the digital platform, write scripts, create graphics, and organize the project.

5. Inventory

I can think of few things that are more tedious and time-wasting for an entrepreneur than analyzing and ordering inventory over and over again. It's normal to need to dive in and sort out your system before handing it off to someone else. But instead, hire an inventory and fulfillment center to handle all of the details for you and streamline the process.

Mishandling inventory can also lead to poor customer service and fulfillment issues. It's never a good idea to try to box up orders and ship them out in the middle of the night.

6. Content Marketing

It can take years to figure out how to connect with the right audience and optimize that marketing for growth. Start with content marketing as a low barrier entry point to connect with your customers. For example, selling an ebook can help establish your authority and credibility while generating more income for your own business. I've personally found this method effective and have sold 40,000 copies of my ebook while generating leads for my businesses.

If writing isn't your expertise, then outsource it. Find a content marketer who can create the type of copy that converts to help educate, inspire, and generate leads for your business.

7. Financial Analysis

You may not have enough money to hire a talented CFO and retain this person on your staff, but that doesn't mean you can't outsource that task or hire someone on retainer to work a set number of hours each month. Your virtual CFO, or someone who comes into the office every few weeks, can review your financials and bookkeeping to ensure your company is in good health and staying on track for success.

Consider the alternative. Skimping on a quality CFO could mean a failure to understand or foresee a financial disaster on the horizon. Avoiding that fate could make the cost of outsourcing a worthy investment.

PART II
GROWTH HACKS FOR YOUR MARKETING—REFLECTIONS

One thing you might have noticed about all the authors so far is while they may be talking about growth hacks, they never talk about how easy it is. No one pretends that they have *the* secret or *the* silver bullet that's going to solve all your growth woes.

Growth hacking is about working smarter—not harder. But make no mistake: It's still hard work. It's not something you can simply farm out to an employee or a consultant. It's a way of thinking about your business and how you run your company.

It's not necessarily immediate, either. Some of UGG founder Brian Smith's growth hacks took a few years to come to fruition. You'll also notice that most of these ideas aren't one-offs—something you can pull the trigger on and then wait around to accrue the benefits. Quite the contrary. Many of these are time-intensive processes that evolve over the course of implementation.

But do they feel it's worth it? Absolutely.

GROWTH HACKING RELATIONSHIPS

"Growth hacking your relationships" might sound like a new way to say Ponzi scheme, but the term best captures the essence of part three. "Relationships" include how you interact with your customers so they become raving fans and evangelists for you, how to leverage strategic partnerships for rapid business growth, and even how to redirect a business model altogether away from users and to referrals.

One thing you'll hear virtually every successful entrepreneur say: they relied on relationships to get where they are. At the core of every business, relationships are your real asset. If you don't have a real connection with your customers, what's to keep them from switching to your competitors? If you don't have basic trust and respect among your team members, how can you effectively work together? If you lose your investors' confidence, it probably won't matter how great your next idea is.

Everything come backs to how we work with other people. If you have great relationships, then building on them to rapidly grow and expand your business shouldn't be a big challenge.

THE COMPANY THAT STOPPED SELLING TO ITS CUSTOMERS

Lydia Belanger

"I wish I had known about this a month ago!" That's what many new customers said about Updater in its early days when it launched in 2010. They'd find out about the product, a software platform that allows people to keep track of their to-do list before moving, but often just a few days before their move date. By then, they had already taken care of setting up new utilities, changing their addresses, and many of the other hassles moving requires. Having access to Updater earlier could have kept them better organized and saved them hours of time.

"We could still help them," says Updater founder and CEO David Greenberg of these late-to-the-game customers, "but we couldn't be as helpful to them."

While the company's executives were grappling with this issue, they spoke with leaders in the real estate industry. They learned that property management companies, real estate brokerages, and others in the space were struggling to help their clients and residents through the moving process. These players wanted to extend their services beyond just finding new homes for their clients.

By teaming up, both sides could create a win-win solution for everyone. Updater wanted to connect with more customers—and connect with them earlier in order to give those customers the best possible experience with its product. Real estate brokerages, property management companies, relocation services, and others in the space wanted to better serve their clients by helping them find trustworthy moving companies and keep track of moving tasks—in turn, bolstering client relationships.

The Fix

To solve its customer acquisition problem and attract users en masse, Updater adopted a new mindset. Although its product serves movers, the real estate industry, relocation services, and even universities are now its direct customers.

The company began establishing partners and licensing its software directly to them. This meant that as of February 2015, the general public could not access Updater without a referral. The invite-only model gives Updater's paying partners an advantage and adds an element of exclusivity given that their clients cannot use the tool without their help.

Partnerships took time to establish. In 2013, Updater had just five partners in the real estate space. In 2014, Updater had 55, and by the end of 2015, that number jumped to 225. As of today, Updater doesn't release the exact number, but it has more than 660 across all 50 states, and the company says it adds an average of 30 more partners every quarter with "nearly no churn."

Updater allows its partners to co-brand the interface so that the software is customized. For example, agents can upload their photo, personalize their profile, and check in with clients. Clients also can find localized information about the best moving services and utilities in their area.

For those who want to benefit from Updater's services but don't have a referral, they can request one on Updater's website. If that avenue doesn't work, Updater provides free content for movers to help them avoid common moving pitfalls, know what questions to ask their real estate agent, discover trustworthy moving companies, and more.

The Result

Throughout 2014 and into the first quarter of 2015, the number of moves being processed through Updater was growing at a good pace. It leaped from 1,126 transactions to 4,559 (more than 300 percent growth in a year). But it wasn't until the model changed in the second quarter of 2015 that Updater saw a huge spike. A couple of months after the company pivoted to invite-only, the number of moves being processed jumped to 38,502—more than 700 percent from the previous quarter.

"We were able to simultaneously onboard five or ten pretty big partners all of a sudden because we finally went live with that integration platform," Greenberg says. "There was almost a waitlist, if you will, of partners who wanted to get on the platform but couldn't because we had not yet finished building the integration platform."

The number of quarterly moves has continued to grow to 535,782 during Q2 2017. This is nearly a 1,300 percent increase from when the company pivoted the model two years ago. Today, Updater self-reports that it processes 11.68 percent of all U.S. moves. Partners refer clients to Updater an average of three to ten weeks in advance of their move dates.

For other businesses wondering whether an invite-only model is right for them, Greenberg suggests asking yourself where your customers are, and whether there are other businesses "a bit further up the food chain" who can be the liaisons between you and your end users. He also notes that he's gotten inquiries from companies in the estate planning and funeral industries—"other technology companies that are focused on a life event"—about how to apply the model.

Another Take

Updater can't just onboard new partners and expect them to do all of the work, of course. Maintaining such relationships is crucial to foster loyalty in the face of potential competition. Plus, the company has to check in regularly to make sure that those partners are getting their clients to take full advantage of the platform and that those clients are having a positive experience, explains Bill Cates, president of Referral Coach International and author of *Beyond Referrals*.

"You're asking this partner, this other firm, to promote this tool. It's a value added, it's nice, their clients or customers probably appreciate it, but is it promoted well enough? Is it ongoing? Is it embedded in parts of their website or other ways that they communicate?" Cates says. "If someone was thinking of borrowing this idea or adopting it to their world, that's one of the key things—to be very clear on what the expectations are. How are you going to measure it? Obviously, there are tracking mechanisms, and you can figure out which traffic is coming from which source."

As Greenberg explains, the largest team of employees within Updater is its client success team, which manages relationships with its partners and tracks closely to make sure that they're getting a return on investment—that Updater is helping them generate referrals, retain clients, or improve resident satisfaction. Updater not only reminds its partners of how it's helping them, but also uses this information to learn what's working well and what's not.

18

WHAT SMALL BRANDS DO THAT BIG NAMES CAN'T

Adam Elder

Benji Wagner knows a dirty little secret about the outdoor apparel industry. Big brands like Patagonia and The North Face may advertise their gear being put to the test in the highest mountains and at the ends of the Earth, but 83 percent of all camping trips in the United States actually take place within a few feet of a car or a house. So Wagner is going straight to those consumers—

people who want to feel comfortable inside a tent perhaps just a few feet above sea level.

"The outdoor industry was founded on mountaineering, but most people are wearing their jacket to go grocery shopping," says Wagner, cofounder and creative director of Poler Outdoor Stuff, which, since its 2011 launch, now sees double-digit growth every year. "The industry went down the rabbit hole in terms of creating more and more technical products for a consumer that's essentially a weekend warrior. Poler makes a great jacket, but we're not going to pretend you're going to climb Mount Everest in it."

It may have once seemed impossible to go up against giant, established brands, but that increasingly just isn't the case. Poler, and the apparel industry at large, tells an important story that's true across all types of businesses. Broad but overlooked segments of consumers are being forgotten by big brands' mass appeal, and even the smallest of players can use the internet to build strong personal connections with those left behind. The key is to tell seductive, inspiring (yet realistic!) stories that resonate and to give customers what the biggest companies can't: a sense of, "Yeah—we get you."

"What many brands have nowadays is the ability to communicate who and what they are," says

Marshal Cohen, a retail analyst with The NPD Group. "Customers today are not looking to be one of a million people—they're looking to be one in a million. They want to stand out."

Communicating that doesn't require big-budget money. Tracksmith, an upscale running apparel brand from Wellesley, Massachusetts, doubled its social media reach in the past ten months with less than $5,000 in ad spending, and has netted a $4.1 million investment from Pentland Group, which owns a stake in Speedo and licenses for Lacoste footwear and Ted Baker. Here's how: It saw that household names like Nike, Adidas, and Puma have conflated running with health and wellness in an effort to win the attention of gym rats—so Tracksmith, which launched in 2011, celebrated the tradition of running as a stand-alone sport. It chased the habitual runner, creating a visceral brand story with photography that portrays everyday runners training, sweating, and looking exhausted rather than triumphant.

"Running apparel originally lacked any sense of style or substance," says cofounder Matt Taylor, a former distance runner at Yale University. "Brands lost touch with the sport and the core culture, and created a much broader message. That's fantastic and has gotten a lot of people off the couch, but it's also left this big void for people who have a deeper connection to running."

To serve those people, Tracksmith created more classic designs that are simple and functional, the opposite of what Taylor calls "the Power Ranger look" of most running apparel.

Small brands are inherently closer to their customers, and that can create all sorts of advantages. Sure, Nike can afford LeBron James as a spokesman, but smaller brands can simply recruit their own users for marketing.

"Niche brands provide a forum for people to share in the story," says The NPD Group's Cohen. "It's that testimonial piece of the puzzle that comes from the user—not the brand itself. Customers don't want to hear you brag about your brand; they want people who've used your product to brag about the brand."

The lingerie company Lively, in fact, crafted its entire brand around its customers. Founder and CEO Michelle Cordiero Grant spent five years at Victoria's Secret overseeing the underwear behemoth's digital merchandising strategy for its core lingerie lines. "At Victoria's Secret, everything feels very focused around how males are really viewing women," Grant says. "Lively is about creating something that's made by women for women, really thinking about how a woman is going to feel in it and what that product does for her mindset in terms of confidence, power, and comfort."

After raising $1.5 million in funding ahead of Lively's April launch, Grant found more than 50 women—not supermodels—based on their passion and aesthetics as seen on their Instagram accounts and enlisted them as ambassadors of the brand's designs, a hybrid of activewear, swimwear, and traditional lingerie. A refer-a-friend email campaign could earn ambassadors purchasing credit if they mentioned the brand or linked to Lively's website. The email-collection campaign was so successful, it exceeded its three-week goal by more than 400 percent in just 48 hours and crashed Lively's site. The brand is now enjoying double-digit sales growth every month.

Some small brands, like Lively and Tracksmith, sell direct online. But when entrepreneurs take their wares out into stores, they're finding another benefit to being a counterweight to big brands. They get to say, "We're not just coming in and trying to take business away from another brand you already have." That's Wagner's pitch for Poler; he stresses that his brand will bring new people into a store because he's serving young people and millennials whom nobody else is. It's working: Poler is carried in Nordstrom, Urban Outfitters, and more than 500 other stores in 30 countries selling right alongside the big brands he competes against.

TWO LESSONS FROM THE AMAZON-WHOLE FOODS MERGER

Per Bylund

Whether or not you're bullish about Amazon's acquisition of Whole Foods Market, you and I can agree that the $13.7 billion price tag was colossal. It wasn't Amazon's first step into the food arena, but it was certainly one of the company's biggest moves to date. And the staggering purchase price wasn't the only fascinating aspect of the deal.

Amazon will acquire the upscale grocery chain of more than 460 stores across the United States,

Canada, and the U.K. In fiscal year 2016, Whole Foods reported about $16 billion in sales.

Unlike most businesses—and particularly large corporations—Amazon refuses to adhere to an industry-specific paradigm. In looking to acquire new components in various markets, Amazon is defying common expectations that many companies treat as hard and fast rules.

It's easy to compare two grocery stores or chains and examine that competition within the confines of their industry. In reality, though, all sellers and producers go head-to-head to secure consumer spending. The intense competition that results takes place across market lines and is no longer industry-specific—if it ever was.

And Amazon and Whole Foods? That blockbuster deal demonstrates the true essence of innovation and competition as it pertains to entrepreneurship.

A Match Made in Heaven

Amazon's purchase of Whole Foods Market is a fascinating move, though it might not change either company the way some suspect.

Many people have a somewhat narrow view of innovation. Society thinks innovative ideas must involve either a revolutionary concept or novel solution to a longstanding problem. Amazon's purchase of Whole Foods is not a new way of doing anything, but it will allow the two companies to combine their capabilities in unique ways.

In short, I don't expect operations at Whole Foods Market to change much. The food chain won't suddenly become the low-price place to stock up on organic groceries. Whole Foods Market will continue to operate under its own name and remain a separate unit within Amazon.

As evidence of that prediction, look to the 2017 press release in which Amazon founder and CEO Jeff Bezos praised the service Whole Foods has been delivering to its loyal customers for nearly four decades. "They're doing an amazing job," Bezos said. "We want that to continue."

That said, Amazon will undoubtedly pair its unique capabilities—wholesale-level organization and consumer-level delivery logistics—with the grocer's strengths: local presence, reputation for high-quality foods, and existing supply contracts.

Amazon will add its own strengths: the ability to streamline farm-to-store logistics while adding a layer of service between Whole Foods' stores and consumers via quick, cost-efficient delivery. Once you consider Amazon's numerous experiments and ventures, the possibilities seem limitless.

For example, Amazon has put a lot of effort into Amazon Prime Air, a delivery system that uses drones to fly orders to customers. Imagine a scenario in which Whole Foods and Amazon fly farm-fresh eggs and produce directly to your breakfast table. This scenario would have seemed unimaginable just a few weeks ago, but the marriage of Amazon and Whole Foods creates a myriad of fascinating opportunities.

Considering the potential for innovation, the entrepreneurial community should be watching Amazon and Whole Foods with bated breath to see the revolutionary retail repercussions sure to come.

Entrepreneurs can learn three major lessons from the deal.

1. Accept Uncertainty as a Prerequisite

Seventy-five percent of respondents in Deloitte's *M&A Trends 2016* survey said they believed that merger and acquisition activity would increase in 2017. The same survey found that 64 percent of respondents also thought that the sizes of these deals would increase.

The problem with bold business moves is that the future is never certain. Whether entrepreneurs create something new through M&A or by starting a company from scratch, they deal with a tremendous amount of uncertainty. They must anticipate the future conditions of a market and position themselves and their businesses accordingly.

When ventures do pan out, the entrepreneurs behind them can use those profits to innovate and provide value to consumers. But nothing here is a guaranteed "sure thing."

Even someone who enjoyed tremendous success in the past is capable of falling flat on his face the next time around. We're talking here about Jeff Bezos, of course. He's achieved incredible things with Amazon—taking on bricks-and-mortar retail juggernauts such as Walmart and Target. But his past success is irrelevant as it relates to the Whole Foods merger. We still don't know what Bezos has in mind with his latest gambit, and there's no guarantee it will be a success.

2. Even Perfect Deals Aren't Perfect

With nearly all mergers and acquisitions, compatibility and potential synergies often look great on paper. Instead of simply adding one capability to another, businesses must merge corporate cultures, unite and streamline information channels, reset the boundaries of decision-making processes, and change how people think about the business and their understanding of what "needs to be done."

That's all well and good. But many M&A deals fail because the cultural and operative obstacles are simply too difficult to overcome. Business leaders are increasingly aware of the essential role culture plays in a company's success. In fact, 87 percent of respondents in Deloitte's 2016 *Human Capital Trends report* recognized the importance of organizational culture. When entrepreneurs take the tremendous step of merging with another business, they should always factor in the costs associated with achieving various synergies.

3. Steel Yourself for Regulatory Headaches

Entrepreneurs will always have to deal with government regulations and restrictions—and not always for good reason. A 2016 survey by Herbert Smith Freehills and Mergermarket found that 71 percent of executives polled blamed competition regulators for their failed deals.

If governments continue to introduce regulations that force internet-based retailers to play by the same rules as bricks-and-mortar stores, it's uncertain whether the union of Amazon and Whole Foods Market will be profitable.

I suspect we might see more federal and state regulations that seek to limit interstate trade. For instance, many states already have rather outrageous regulations regarding alcohol sales. And, then, quite a few states use a three-tier system that requires producers, wholesalers, and retailers to be different actors (and sometimes the last two must be based in the state). Similar restrictions could hamstring the Amazon-Whole Foods partnership before it gets traction.

Considering that Whole Foods has hundreds of stores in several countries, Amazon will also have to maneuver its way through international trade regulations, international supply chains, and so on. The answers aren't yet apparent—in many ways, even the questions are still unknown—and the learning process will likely be expensive. Entrepreneurs considering a move into uncharted territory should keep an eye on Amazon's progress to learn from the company's successes and failures.

Any significant investment carries a decent amount of risk. Time will tell whether Amazon's decision to acquire Whole Foods was a brilliant move or a ridiculous blunder. Either way, entrepreneurs should watch this merger as it unfolds. If all ends well, they'll enjoy the consumer perks like anyone else. They'll be able to get fresh, organic snacks delivered straight to their doorsteps.

If the merger goes poorly, however, at least those entrepreneur and consumers will learn some valuable lessons along the way.

TEN STEPS TO FORMING LONG-LASTING STRATEGIC PARTNERSHIPS

Michel Koopman

From small company owners to enterprise executives, partnerships are a delicate yet necessary part of any successful business strategy.

The most important thing to know about partnerships is that they are not easy, nor do they always work out. That is why it is critical to vet out the potential partner as much as possible during the discovery period, as the overarching goal is to produce a mutually beneficial relationship while fulfilling the objectives and missions of each organization involved.

During the initial talks with a potential partner, there must be three opportunities available: leverage, scalability, and incremental revenue. First, the partner must have a strategic market presence, brand, or product that you can leverage from. Next, the engagement must be repeatable and able to be rolled out across sales forces. Finally, an opportunity to increase revenue must be present. Without the presence of all three, simply move on.

If the above requirements are met, then the partnership can begin to develop.

Here are ten guidelines that all successful alliances that drive meaningful revenue must meet over the course of the collaboration.

1. Business Alignment

Define a strategic mutual vision of success for the parties involved. Once the partners agree on what success looks like for both sides and how each can leverage the strengths of the other, then the foundation is established.

Without setting clear expectations upfront, you're setting yourself up for disappointment or even disaster. So often, entrepreneurs waste months or even years trying to make relationships work that they never should have entered in the first place.

2. Agreement and Contracts

It is important to document, often contractually, many of the details of the partnership, such as the type of relationship, responsibilities, mutual risks, rewards, payments, service level agreements, branding guidelines, rules of engagement, and more for both parties. Of course, the extent and kind of details depend on the type of partnership (e.g., joint marketing, product development, reseller, referral, etc.).

How many times have you had someone agree to something and then weeks later you find yourselves disagreeing on what was said? That's why "getting it in writing" is so crucial, especially when it comes to business partnerships. You want a common point of reference.

3. Business Planning

Each party must collaborate to create a business plan. At set time intervals, make sure this strategy remains relevant and in line with the endgame. The business plan should clearly state missions, objectives, and revenue goals.

You and your partner may have the same goals only to discover you had very different ideas about how to achieve those goals. The act of working together to walk through your plan step by step gives you the chance to understand each other better and ensure you're on the same page as you begin to put your plan into action.

4. Executive Engagement

Senior executives are the main influencers, and it is imperative they are on board with the partnership vision. They must be well connected to their counterparts and regularly communicate the overall alliance goals.

This is where the rubber meets the road. Do the people who put the plan into action actually buy into the whole idea? Or do some of them simply pay lip service because they don't believe in the partnership in the first place?

5. Product Integration

Both parties must ensure and communicate (in time) that both products and/or services work seamlessly together. Clients should feel confident about the commitment of both companies behind their joint solution. This may require quite an amount of due diligence on your part beforehand. The last thing you want to hear is that all of your hard work has been for nothing because the technology can't work together—a non-starter that should have been discovered early on.

6. Marketing

The world needs to know about the partnership. Strategic and consistent communication needs to be conveyed throughout the alliance both internally and externally. The partnership creates a joint-value proposition unique to customers, and it needs to be conveyed through marketing content and leads. Don't overlook the employees and other people inside the partnership. If your internal teams don't fully understand the partnership, it's almost a sure bet your customers don't, either.

7. Field Readiness

The sales teams of all partnered companies—whether they be direct, channel, agents, or something else—must be well-versed on the collaboration with a consistent message. Each salesperson should be equipped with the necessary tools to effectively verbalize and demonstrate the partnership. In other words, one-way communication isn't enough. Your customer-facing employees need to be equipped and trained to have two-way conversations with customers to explain the partnership's benefits to them and how they can take advantage of them.

8. Compensation

Will sales professionals, partner managers, and executives be financially rewarded if the partnership is successful? Is individual success aligned with corporate success? One of the best ways to ensure a successful partnership is to allow key players to share in its success.

9. Sales Engagement

From field representatives to managers, make sure the sales teams are on the same page. Some questions to ask: Are they collaborating? Is there a target list actively being worked? If so, which party is working it? Is there a pipeline review?

Circling back to point number seven: Are they prepared to have on-the-spot conversations with customers? Can you provide a handy Q&A sheet or talking points for them to refer to? Do the salespeople and their managers have an incentive to push the partnership's opportunities?

10. Governance

You will have to decide how often the success of the partnership will be put under review. Will these reviews be a regular occurrence? If so, how will these review meetings take place? You can opt for weekly meetings or calls with partner managers, quarterly meetings with vice presidents, or whatever you think may be appropriate. Ideally, you would spend more time in the beginning as you work out the challenges and then less time as things progress and routines become established.

This is an ongoing, living process, and it does take time to reach full maturity, so do not expect all the pieces to fall into place on the first day. The best partnerships can take weeks, months, or even years to cultivate into their maximum potential. Although it does take time, a truly great partnership is worth the effort. Remember, you are partnering for a reason—together, you are better than alone.

Leverage this, grow it, and drive new business opportunities!

21

RELATIONSHIPS ARE WHAT LEVERAGE HARD WORK INTO SUCCESS

Gerard Adams

Every successful entrepreneur knows that relationships are key. No business is made in a vacuum. The way you interact with clients, employees, coworkers, and other entrepreneurs can give your business life or bring it to its death.

Unfortunately, there's no perfect how-to for building the right kind of relationships. For example, you could meet someone who could potentially become a huge client for your startup.

However, saying the wrong thing at the wrong time, or possibly even having poor body language, can end the relationship before it even starts.

Entrepreneurs also have to be concerned about who they're building relationships with. If your largest client is somebody you can't trust, then you need to ask yourself: is our business safe with this person? Putting your faith in the wrong people can put your business in a pretty tough spot.

With all this in mind, there's little chance that you'll get very far without some good connections. You never know what a connection can offer, and the bigger your network, the better.

Engaging with Others

One of the first things you'll need to do after you start a business—and likely even before you start a business—is connection building. Finding the right connections can help you and your business succeed. But where do you find these connections, and once you find them, how do you form the relationship?

The best way to find good connections is through networking. There are plenty of ways to approach this: you could ask your friends and family if they have anyone who could help you, you could research possible connections on your own, or you could go to networking events.

If you aren't good at networking, then don't let this step deter you. Not many people are born ready to network, and building a real business connection with a complete stranger can be a difficult process. But practice makes perfect. Besides, these are connections you'll need to succeed. You can't afford to let these people slip away. If you're quick to adapt, then you'll quickly learn the ins and outs of networking. If not, there are plenty of helpful guides around the internet that can give you tips.

Building Value

One tip I can give to those who aren't the best at networking: Be valuable.

Just take a moment to understand how the entire process of networking works. Normally, it will be you and a complete stranger. There's a good chance that you want or need something from them or someone they know, which means that they're valuable to you.

If you walk up to this person and immediately ask them to give something to you, what do you think they'll say? If they say yes, then you've found one of the most generous people in the world. If they say no, then you've met a rational human being.

When a stranger walks up to you and asks you to listen to their business pitch, asks for the contact of someone you know, or asks for funding, your normal response would be "no." In all honesty, this should be your reaction. After all, you're not going to give up something important to a stranger just because they asked.

The same works when you're networking. Recognize that whoever you want to approach is a person, and that you're a stranger to them. Make yourself valuable. When you approach them, try to build a genuine connection. Ask them about their business and their goals, and if you're at a networking event, ask them why they came. Everyone who goes to a networking event is looking for something; if you can help them out, then they'll be much more likely to help you out.

If they aren't looking for anything, perhaps they'll learn something about you during a normal conversation. If you build a connection with them, they'll be more likely to help you with what you need.

Working with Other Entrepreneurs

One of the greatest parts about entrepreneurship is that it's always changing. This keeps things dynamic, sure, but it also means that the field is constantly innovating, and innovation is good.

An innovation that I've noticed going on is in the interconnectivity of entrepreneurs. Entrepreneurs are becoming more likely to work with each other instead of against each other.

This is happening because entrepreneurs understand the importance of relationships. Every relationship you build is a connection that could help you down the road. If I were to connect with an entrepreneur who wanted me to help get them exposure, then I'm immediately proving myself valuable to them. This increases the chances of them helping me if I need to tap into their network.

Just remember that you can be valuable to anyone—you just need to prove it to them. If you want to have someone help you, help them first. The more you do for others, the more they'll do for you.

People are built to work together in a community, and a network is no different.

PART III
GROWTH HACKING RELATIONSHIPS—REFLECTIONS

As we said in the introduction to this section: everything comes back to relationships.

In the digital era—and especially when talking about growth hacking—the idea of using our connections with other individuals as the basis for great growth seems antiquated.

But as these authors have demonstrated, there is plenty of opportunity for enterprising business owners who know how to use what they have. Growth hacking your relationships isn't about abusing those connections; it is quite the reverse. It's about using the trust and mutual respect you have with others to benefit you both and leverage the growth potential just waiting to be used.

HACKING YOUR INDUSTRY FOR GROWTH

I n trying to find common ground among all these authors, one thing most agree on is that you can growth hack any business. The following articles and stories certainly make the case for that.

House rehab, fashion design, global HR—it can be done. But the big question is: why? Why hack an industry if you can just go with the flow and plug along? Well, it's simple, really. Hacking your growth means that you are all in, ready to take your business to a level beyond the everyday standard operating procedure. When you do that, when you maximize your ability to grow and scale, then you not only separate your business from the pack, but you also ignite creativity—in yourself, in your team, and in your industry. The moves you make to achieve next-level growth don't just impact your immediate universe; they ripple out to other businesses who pick up where you leave off, setting the next trend, and so on.

If you think that your industry can't be growth hacked, we promise you that someone, somewhere is figuring out how to do exactly that . . . and that unless you also embrace the idea that you can, too, you'll soon be sitting around wondering, *Now, why didn't I think of that?*

You absolutely can growth hack your industry, and you should. You just have to find out how.

WHY YOU SHOULD FOCUS ON "DIFFERENT" AND "BETTER," NOT "MORE"

Jess Ekstrom

As an entrepreneur, you're expected to be the CEO, the operations officer, the graphic designer, the marketer, the accountant, and any other hat you can possibly fit on your head.

You're programmed to not just do everything but also to do *more* . . . and to worry about what others are doing, too.

In fact, it's easy to peek your head outside and see what other businesses in your industry are doing to compare your own efforts. But every time you do, you discover one more thing you're not doing that someone else is.

Is your business on Snapchat? Do you host staff retreats? Does your business have a brand-rep program? Do your shipping envelopes have your logo imprinted on them? Do you exhibit at trade shows? Do you have flash sales of your product? The questions go on and on.

On one hand, it's great to draw inspiration from others and develop new ideas for your company. But on the other, it's important to understand the difference between doing *more* and doing *different.*

Forget "More"

Always feeling that you can and should be doing more with your business can be toxic. You may spread your company too thin; you may have one finger on every one of the bases but not have the ability to prevent any of those bases from drifting off-mission.

Worse, by trying to do everything, you diffuse your focus and lose sight of the important things. On top of that, your relentless obsession with more, more, more inserts itself into the culture of your company. If you never feel that you're doing enough and that the competition is passing you by, you can be sure that your team is feeling the pressure, too.

Focus on "Better"

Instead of always feeling that you should do more, think about doing something better.

What have you already implemented at your company? What could you do better with it? For example, my company donates a headband to a child with cancer for every headband we sell. And we're continuing to do more. We recently improved our customers' donation experience by providing a donation confirmation email specifying what hospital their headbands has gone to. We took a system that was already working well within our business and made it even better.

Another example is Starbucks. The coffee giant has had its rewards system in place for a while: with its system, customers' points are tallied on their gift cards. But when the company integrated rewards with its app, that move allowed customers to reload their card, check their points, and even pay for their order straight from their phones. The point system was still the same; Starbucks just designed a better way for customers to utilize it.

Every time you do something new—getting on a new social media platform or embarking on a new campaign ad—you're essentially starting at the bottom of the learning curve. Like any process, it takes time to work out the details and start to reap the benefits.

Something as simple as having your logo on your outgoing envelopes involves a number of details. Who's going to print it? Should you use a local printer or find one for cheaper online? Should you just have your logo on regular-sized envelopes, or should you have a variety of sizes? Would it be cost-effective to use label stickers, or would that cheapen your brand? If you really want your mail to stand out and make a statement, should you go with a high-grade of paper for your envelopes?

Instead of chasing after every new idea, why not refocus on your current systems and put your efforts toward something that already exists and simply making it a little better?

Here's another twist on the topic. "More" usually means "new," but new doesn't always mean better. There may be a cool new social media platform that came online yesterday, but is it really better than the social media platforms you already use? Your competition may have a new gizmo, but is it benefitting them? Or is it just a shiny new toy that's going to lose its cool factor in a few weeks?

Don't chase more; chase better.

Focus on "Different"

I read a book called *Zag* by Marty Neumeier. The idea the book presents is that when everyone else zigs, your business should zag. It's not about doing more or better—it's about doing different. The book encourages companies to find the "white space" they can fill in and position themselves with the intro, "Our _____ is the only _____ that _____."

Can you fill in that blank? If not, think about what you might do "different" at your company that no one else in your industry does.

Headbands of Hope is the *only* company that donates headbands to kids with cancer. Southwest Airlines is the *only* company with no assigned seats. ClassPass is the *only* company that allows you one membership to various gyms. Batch is the *only* retail company that delivers an authentic taste of select Southern cities.

You get the picture.

When you're substantially different from your competition, and especially when you're the *only* _____ that _____, you don't have to necessarily do more. In fact, doing more might detract from your efforts to be different. If you're always trying to keep up with the competition, it's just an arms race. Instead, zig when they zag, and zag when they zig.

Dare to be different.

HOW THE DOLLAR SHAVE CLUB DISRUPTED A MULTIBILLION-DOLLAR INDUSTRY

Jaclyn Trop

Michael Dubin, founder of the Dollar Shave Club, occasionally allowed himself to envision the moment when everything paid off. He'd be ushered into a grand ceremony where some conglomerate, eager to own his massively successful company, would offer him a fortune for the pleasure.

"I thought we would pass a really nice pen around in a wood-paneled boardroom with portraits of men with white hair," he says.

When the moment actually came on July 19, 2016, there was none of that. He was in his pajamas lying on a bed at the Skytop Lodge in the Pocono Mountains of Pennsylvania. His lawyers had been working through the night, and now the sun was up and Dubin had his cellphone pressed to his ear. In two hours, he was set to take the stage in the hotel's ballroom, where leaders of the multinational conglomerate Unilever would gather for its biannual conference. There, they'd announce that he was now part of their team: Dollar Shave Club was being acquired for $1 billion. But first, the deal had to be finalized. Dubin listened as, one by one, the executives on the phone gave their approval. Then, it came down to him.

Today, Dubin swears he hadn't been looking to sell the company so early. (He declines to say whether other offers had come along.) The way he saw it, his five-year-old Dollar Shave Club was only getting started. When he launched it in 2012, the razor market was dominated by Gillette, which claimed 72 percent of the U.S. market and had been purchased by Procter & Gamble for $57 billion in 2005. Schick was a distant second. But Dubin saw an opening. He could start by undercutting the big competitors on razors, and then he could build out something that felt less like a shaving supply company and more like a full-scale men's club—a subscription-based grooming brand with personality that men actually identify with.

"If anyone else had brought me the idea, I would have said, 'Well, it's a tough category with lots of global competitors,'" says venture capitalist Kirsten Green, founder of Silicon Valley-based Forerunner Ventures.

But Dubin quickly convinced her to be one of his company's early investors. Spend any time with Dubin and it's easy to understand why. Tall, sandy-haired and preppy, the 38-year-old entrepreneur can vacillate between guy's-guy sarcasm and serious, intense shop talk. He's also a voracious reader, giving every new employee copies of two of his favorite books: Thich Nhat Hanh's *How to Sit* and Peter Drucker's *The Effective Executive*.

"Within the first ten minutes of meeting Michael, I was completely drawn into his idea and vision and him," Green says.

In the years that followed, Dollar Shave Club released a full range of products, made a name for itself with viral online videos, and produced the kind of growth rarely seen in the once sleepy category of men's grooming. Other mail-order companies, such as Harry's and ShaveMOB, entered the space, and Amazon got into the game as well. By 2015, four years after Dubin began, web sales for men's shaving gear had more than doubled industry-wide—to $263 million—and the following year, Dollar Shave Club was the number one online razor company with 51 percent of the market (compared with Gillette's 21.2 percent, according to research firm Slice Intelligence). This clearly spooked the industry giant; Gillette launched its own Gillette Shave Club and bought promoted tweets to claim things like "two million guys and counting no longer buy from the other shave clubs." But Dubin's company kept growing, more than doubling its revenue every year since launching, starting with $6 million in 2012 and on track for more than $250 million in subsequent years.

Still, the sale to Unilever was a detour from his initial roadmap. He hadn't built Dollar Shave Club for a quick cash-out. He thought his company could become "a brand that sits on the shelf next to the Starbucks and the Nikes and the Red Bulls of the world," he says, and he wanted to be the one to lead it there. That meant Dollar Shave Club must retain what made it special—its culture, its voice, and its free spirit. But would his then-205 employees and three million-plus members, who were attracted to its lovable scrappiness, still feel that connection once the startup became part of a corporate giant?

"I think it's always a concern of a founder," Dubin says. "The most important aspect of culture is how people feel about their role. You need clear financial and spiritual objectives and benefits. If you don't get that right, it doesn't matter how many beanbag chairs you have."

The company's open floor plan in a Los Angeles suburb doesn't have beanbag chairs at all, actually, but it does have a strong culture of communal fun and a tireless work ethic: free lunch on Tuesday, events like bouquet making on Valentine's Day, and Play-Station and Nintendo boxes beneath a neon sign in pink cursive that says "GET BACK TO WORK." ("That's a bit of our dry humor," says spokeswoman Kristina Levsky.)

Unilever, however, promised that the company he built would stay the same—and he would have the financial freedom to truly achieve his vision. So in the hotel room, still in his pajamas, Dubin flipped open his laptop and brought up DocuSign. The $1 billion contract appeared in front of him. He clicked OK. Sale finalized. Then, DocuSign's standard message popped up: "You're done signing. A copy of this document will be sent to your email address when completed by all signers. You can also download or print using the icons above."

"I took a screenshot," Dubin says, "because it was so unceremonious."

A few hours later, as planned, Dubin went onstage to be introduced as Unilever's newest leader. Then, he and Unilever's president of North American operations, Kees Kruythoff, flew to Los Angeles to tell Dollar Shave Club's employees. As Dubin recalls, "He said, 'Congratulations; you just bought Unilever,' which was his way of saying it was important for us to maintain our culture."

Dubin had taken the company this far. Now, everyone looked to him to keep it going.

Dubin grew up in Bryn Mawr, Pennsylvania, not far from the Pocono Mountains, where he signed that deal of a lifetime. After graduating from Emory University, he moved to New York City where he took several jobs in marketing and advertising, seeking work in the smaller, more nimble business units of companies including NBCUniversal and Time Inc. "I like molten environments that have yet to harden because it allows you the opportunity to have a voice and to shape things, and I do think that I'm a good shaper of things," he says. At night, he took classes in accounting, corporate finance, and comedy improvisation, a combination that helped him see business as a fluid, ever-changing space. "One of the tenets of improv is to use what's given to you and make the most out of it," he says. "You can't be overly precious about the way you had outlined things in your head at the beginning of a venture."

In 2011, Dubin met a friend's father-in-law at a party. Over cocktails, the man told Dubin that he needed to unload a warehouse full of surplus razor blades. Dubin's improv instincts kicked in; he offered to help. Dubin thought about his long-standing irritation with the razor-buying process—go to the store, ask a salesclerk to open the plexiglass-encased "razor fortress," and pay more than seems reasonable for a small pack of blades. If he could mail blades to customers for a lower price, he reasoned, men would appreciate the problem he was solving. And from there, the opportunity only got bigger.

"American men are evolving in their bathroom routine," Dubin says. "Five years ago, if you spent time in front of the mirror, people would have called you a metrosexual. We now live in the age where it's OK to hug guys and compliment and give advice." But while some major brands had shifted to serving those guys—Axe shook off its bro image, Old Spice rebooted its marketing, and Dove launched a line of men's products with a 2010 Super Bowl ad—nobody had tried to build a community around affordable men's grooming products. Dubin thought he could.

He registered the domain dollarshaveclub.com within a week and began sketching out his notion for a grooming empire. A few months later, he quit his job to work on it full-time. And on March 6, 2012, at 6 a.m. Pacific time, he published a video that announced Dollar Shave Club to the world and would establish the voice it always spoke in. It opens on Dubin at a desk, pitching his razors. But then he stands up and walks with a swagger. "Are the blades any good?" he asks. "No." Then he stops next to a sign that says "our blades are f***ing great," and from there, the video turns into a self-aware, shticky, hilariously slapstick pitch, with Dubin wielding a machete, driving a forklift and dancing with a guy in a bear costume while scattering dollar bills into the air with a leaf blower. It cost $4,500 to make, which came out of Dubin's meager savings, and it proved an instant success. The company took 12,000 orders that day. The video has since been watched 24 million times on YouTube.

"It spoke to a psychographic that wants to take life lightly," says Olivier Toubia, a Columbia Business School professor who teaches the video as a case study. "Sometimes, customers just want something simple." This was an audience that the likes of Gillette had overlooked with its self-serious high-tech blades and vibrating handles. And Dubin, relying on the insights he'd learned by working in marketing, intentionally timed the release for maximum impact—just before South By Southwest when reporters were in a lull waiting for big digital news to break. He coupled the video's launch with the announcement that his company had closed $1 million in seed funding, so, Dubin says, "the tech press picked it up first, and then the mainstream press picked it up from there. At that point, it was viral."

Even at the start, when Dollar Shave Club was functionally a one-man operation selling surplus blades, Dubin wanted to pay off on the "club" part. What could he offer aside from a mail-order product? He decided to designate himself the company's first "Club Pro." It was a spin on customer service; rather than just helping people with their orders, a Club Pro would be on hand to answer any grooming questions—a kind of on-call concierge available by email, phone, text, online chat, or social media. If a man somewhere wondered why his skin was red on the days he didn't shave, Dubin would find the answer.

Once Dubin hired a few employees, he and a small team began traveling the country to learn more about people's grooming habits. They focused on regional events like the Maine Lobster Festival and the Gilroy Garlic Festival—places where grooming conversations weren't exactly the norm. The point was to meet average guys on their turf and learn what they wanted. "We figured out how to talk to people—not at them," says Cassie Jasso, one of the company's first ten hires.

Dubin was eager to expand into other products, but the festivals taught him that he couldn't just start stocking his digital shelves. Men were happy to talk about grooming, but they weren't always knowledgeable or adventurous about it. To succeed, Dollar Shave Club would have to be more than a voice—it would have to be the leader of a conversation and an educator that men actually wanted to hear from.

At 10 a.m. on a Tuesday morning, Dubin is presiding over a glass-enclosed conference room in the modern, low-slung warehouse in Marina del Rey, California, that Dollar Shave Club has occupied since 2015. Eight members of the company's creative team have convened for a brainstorming session; they want to script a video that explains their sulphate-free soap and hairstyling products.

The company has expanded into more than 30 products across five categories and promoted them with hundreds of funny videos for TV, YouTube, and its own website. Dubin still stars in some, but other staffers get camera time as well. Today, the group considers Fadi Mourad, the company's gregarious, tattooed chief innovation officer who is responsible for developing new products.

"What if we dressed Fadi as Clippy from Microsoft?" someone suggests, and then makes his voice squeaky to impersonate the software's much-maligned paper clip mascot. "Hmm … looks like you're buying shampoo!"

They run through several more scenarios: Fadi as mad scientist, Fadi as zany Swedish chef. Someone proposes a cooking show format where Fadi shows how shave butter is made.

"Bingo," Dubin says. "I love that. I think that's a really fun format to play with. I like the juxtaposition of the scientist with the average guy. That cuts to the heart of the brand and who we are."

That sense of brand—and of what people expect from it—has steered not just the company's marketing but its product development as well. It took Mourad some time to adjust to it. He had spent 15 years developing products for Estée Lauder and Bumble & Bumble and was used to long meetings where trend forecasters would dissect runway shows and fashion magazines. "My first executive meeting here was eye-opening because nobody cared what those trends were," says Mourad. Instead, the company often turned to regular guys to see what they needed, what they were excited to try, and what basics could be improved upon. "That's never how I would have started the innovation process anywhere else."

Much like its foray into oddball festivals, Dollar Shave Club began this process with a lot of small consumer panels. "We talk through the 'shit, shave, and shower' routine with our customers and uncover pain points," Mourad says. Surprising ideas would come out of these, like when one panel began complaining about rough toilet paper. From this, the company created its popular One Wipe Charlies, a flushable, moist cloth it bills as the "#1 way to clean up after #2." "No trend would have told you that guys are looking for butt wipes," Mourad says. (Meanwhile, when beard oils and dry shampoos briefly became a thing, Dollar Shave Club passed; its panels just didn't seem interested.) This saves Dollar Shave Club a lot of hassle. About 80 percent of the products it tries out eventually make it to market.

Of course, this doesn't mean the company always hits the bull's-eye. Last year, it launched an exfoliating cloth marketed to men as a "shower tool," but the reviews weren't great. "We didn't hide the reaction," says chief marketing officer Adam Weber, who previously worked at Procter & Gamble and Gilt Groupe. "We had a very transparent conversation with our customers and redesigned it in less than two weeks." Then, they sent a refund to all 64,000 members who bought the old version even if they hadn't asked for one.

"That was the moment we realized we needed a much bigger member panel," Weber says. Its other panels had helped products develop, but Dollar Shave Club had no way of testing products once they actually existed. Last year, it created a 500-member, invite-only group of long-standing customers. They now test new products and give instant feedback, which Weber says has helped the company overall. "It creates a sense of urgency to react faster," he says.

For the three million-plus customers who aren't in that little group, Dollar Shave Club is continually seeking ways to engage them with more than just sales pitches. It has hired writers and editors to create MEL, an online men's lifestyle magazine; a funny pamphlet called "Bathroom Minutes," which comes in every delivery; and the company's podcast, which tackles topics such as, "Why Is Everyone on the Internet So Angry?" and, "Which Body Parts Can You Actually Grow Back?" And although Dubin long ago stopped having time to personally answer customers' grooming questions, he's replaced himself with more than 100 Club Pros who now work out of the company's headquarters.

In fact, as the company continued to grow, Dubin was increasingly being drawn away from the club members he'd courted. "I went out and raised money every 12 months, which takes three months at the very least and becomes your number one, all-consuming priority," Dubin says. It's something every startup CEO has to deal with, of course. But then an unexpected conversation had him envisioning a very different routine.

In 2015, when Dubin was interviewing investment banks to help raise Series D funding, he met J.P. Morgan managing director Romitha Mally. Shortly after, Mally ran into her friend Kees Kruythoff, president of Unilever's North American operations, at the Virgin Atlantic lounge at Heathrow. "I told him about this amazing company we just raised money for, a 21st-century men's grooming platform with sticky customers," she says.

Intrigued, Kruythoff asked to meet Dubin. The three of them had dinner at the Mandarin Oriental hotel in New York. "There was instant chemistry between the two of them," Mally says. There was synergy between the companies, too. Both men saw the possibilities in combining the resources of a multinational conglomerate with a disruptive innovator. Dubin thought he could recruit Kruythoff to serve in an advisory role or on Dollar Shave Club's board.

Unilever had a bigger vision. Five months after that dinner, Unilever called Mally after seeing Dollar Shave Club's Super Bowl commercial to say it wanted to buy the company. Unilever was especially interested in the company's substantial trove of customer data and potential to scale globally. "Most consumer packaged-goods companies distribute through a retailer, so you never know who your best customers are," Mally says. "But Michael found a powerful way to connect directly with the consumer."

The offer flattered Dubin. And the more he sat with it, the more he liked it. Unilever was offering to keep everything the same: Dubin and his company would stay in Marina del Rey under his leadership. And with Unilever's money, Dubin would be freed up to focus on growing the business at a rate he couldn't have imagined before. "When we began the discussions with Unilever, I thought, 'Wow, what could I do with 25 percent more of my time? What amazing results we could have," Dubin says. "We didn't want to open this up to competitive bidding. At a certain point, it became too attractive to say no."

"Excuse me?" A guy with long hair and a beard bends over our table. "Are you the founder of Dollar Shave Club?" Dubin nods; this happens regularly, ever since his first viral video made him an internet star. "Love what you did with the razors," the guy says, proffering a fist bump before walking away.

We are at Superba Food + Bread, a casual breakfast spot in Dubin's Venice, Californa, neighborhood that he visits most mornings before heading into the office. He knows the secret parking spots and usually has a black coffee waiting for him on the counter. As the man walks away, Dubin sizes up his grooming habits. "He looked like the kind of guy who uses an electric razor," Dubin says. "He had great hair, so he must use our amazing hair products."

Dubin is feeling relaxed these days. He's loving the life of a CEO who doesn't fundraise or worry about running out of money. "The ability for me to focus more completely on operations and running the business has de-stressed me a bit," he says. And he's energized by planning Dollar Shave Club's next big move: international expansion. The company already operates in Canada and Australia, and is now plotting its footprint in Europe and Asia.

New cultures will create new challenges for Dollar Shave Club. After all, the company grew by keenly understanding the American man. Now, it will have to dissect very different cultures with very different grooming standards. But Dubin's team treats this as liberating—allowing it to follow new paths and enter new product categories, all while following the same instincts Dubin used to grow the company in the first place. "Michael can look into the future better than anyone I've ever met," Weber, the CMO, says. "Some people call it luck, but I think Michael has a very good sense of when to do what. There's no set template. You can't go and buy the playbook."

So what's next? The conversations inside Dollar Shave Club may shock the average dude. Hair color. Vitamins. Some are even talking about men's color makeup, something Mourad, the innovation officer, truly believes American men will soon want. But if those guys take a while to come around, that's fine: Dollar Shave Club can now hone those products in more fashion-forward countries. And one day, when guys here are ready for makeup, Dollar Shave Club will probably do what it does best: make a video that transforms a quiet category into something surprisingly special.

24

HOW GLOSSIER HACKED SOCIAL MEDIA TO BUILD A CULT-LIKE FOLLOWING

Alyssa Giacobbe

On a Thursday afternoon in late spring, 32-year-old Glossier founder and CEO Emily Weiss rides the elevator to the penthouse level of her company's downtown Manhattan headquarters. She's a thoroughly millennial girl boss in jeans, sneakers, and a royal blue sweatshirt with "weiss" embroidered in small white script. Her hair is pulled back in a ponytail, and for the founder of a beauty products company, she wears notably little makeup—just some mascara and possibly a swipe of Glossier Lip Gloss, a recent product release touted online as having a "fuzzy doe-foot applicator."

A former teen model, Weiss is beautiful but not intimidating, either by nature or by design (probably a little of both). After all, her company's popularity is directly related to her ability to cultivate a feeling of friendship with and among her customers. Just enough relatability is key.

In the elevator, a short woman in her 50s turns to chat her up.

"Do you work here?" she asks.

"I do!" exclaims Weiss.

"People really love it, I hear," says the woman. "It's my first visit. I work around the corner. I'm Elizabeth."

On 6, the doors open to reveal Elizabeth's destination. It's the Glossier showroom, the brand's only existing retail space, at least for now. It is a floor-through, gut-renovated homage to millennial pink: pink-and-white packaged products arranged on pink lacquered displays, pale-pink-subway-tiled walls, staff dressed in pink mechanics' jumpsuits, fresh-cut pink and white flowers and flattering lighting. It's 5 P.M., and the space is buzzing with a few dozen devoted Glossier fans of varying ages, ethnicities and genders. We're told that Hilary Duff, the actress, has just left. "People really do come here to hang out," says Brittney Ricca, Glossier's manager of communications. She means it. Last summer, someone had a pizza delivered here.

If it weren't already obvious, Glossier inspires a kind of devotion and intrigue unmatched in the traditionally fickle beauty space. In less than three years, and with just 24 products that range in price from $12 to $35, the startup has become one of the industry's biggest disruptors. Weiss won't share figures but says that revenues are up 600 percent year over year and the brand has tripled its active customer count over the past 12 months. Its flagship now does more sales per square foot than the average Apple Store with lines out the door and a very impressive 65 percent conversion rate. And last November, Weiss announced on Glossier's blog that the company had raised $24 million in Series B funding, representing a total $34.4 million in venture capital to date, which will go toward opening additional retail locations, shipping internationally, and expanding product categories. In July, the company announced it would begin shipping to France, the U.K., and Canada, with more countries to come. And soon it will move its headquarters to a new, 26,000-square-foot space at the flashy One SoHo Square in New York (where MAC Cosmetics, an Estée Lauder company, also has an office) and add 282 new jobs to its current team of 85, funded in part by a $3 million tax credit from the state of New York.

The day before, Glossier had released its latest hotly anticipated product: Invisible Shield, introduced to the Glossier community as "a sunscreen that doesn't suck." It was inspired by persistent customer calls for a sunblock that wasn't sticky, greasy, white or tinted, and didn't smell like sunblock. It took two years to create. And it's selling fast. In the past 24 hours, Weiss says, she's gotten "so many DMs from people on Instagram writing to say, 'Thank you so much for listening; we've been waiting for this moment.'"

Weiss writes every one of them back because she, too, has been waiting for this moment, ever since she had an insight years ago that has since bloomed into a corporate philosophy and a runaway success. The beauty product industry has thrived on making women feel bad and selling them overpriced products that don't deliver, but it doesn't have to be that way. Weiss had a different idea, one as simple as it is revolutionary: Make them feel good.

Weiss grew up in Wilton, Connecticut, the older of two children. Her mother stayed home to raise her and her brother; her father worked in sales for Pitney Bowes. "He was very much the American dream—didn't graduate college, printed his own business cards, worked his way up from door-to-door salesman," she says. "I learned the value of hard work from them."

As a teenager, she dabbled in local modeling, did her friends' makeup for prom, and studied fashion and magazines. At 15, she began babysitting for a neighbor who worked for Ralph Lauren, and then tested out her budding hustling skills. "I said, 'I love your kids,'" she recalls, "'but is it too bold for me to say I'd really like to intern where you work?'" It was not. After spending two summers interning at Ralph Lauren, she enrolled at NYU in 2003. Someone at Ralph Lauren introduced her to Amy Astley, then the editor in chief of *Teen Vogue,* and Weiss spent her sophomore through senior years cramming her classes into two days so she could spend the other three interning at the magazine.

Teen Vogue became her first taste of fame. Fans of the MTV reality show *The Hills* might recall the time when "co-stars" Lauren Conrad and Whitney Port, ostensibly interns in the magazine's West Coast office, were pitted against "intern Emily." While reality shows aren't the best representation of reality, Weiss' scripted persona had plenty of truth. She was cast as a type-A New Yorker foil to Conrad and Port's laid-back Valley girls, a preternaturally poised undergrad who knew how to use the word *chinoiserie.* And famously (at least among *Hills* fans), she triumphed. In one episode, Weiss was invited to stay for a fancy dinner that all three interns had helped set up while Conrad and Port were banished to go eat in their cars.

Weiss graduated in 2007 with a degree in studio art, and then kept rising in media. She was a fashion assistant at *W,* then an on-set styling assistant for *Vogue,* where she routinely pumped the biggest talents in fashion for information. ("I was able to ask these women, *What's that lipstick; what's the hair?"*) She also learned that while most women thought a lot about their own beauty regimens, they rarely talked about them.

Weiss suspected this stemmed from an uncomfortable fact: The beauty industry is all but built on telling women, even subtly, that they aren't good enough. Talking openly about using beauty products, therefore, can read as tacit admission of inadequacy, insecurity, vanity, or frivolity. "I found that whenever I used to ask women about their approach to beauty, they would sort of shrink and be like, 'Oh, me? Like, I'm really low-maintenance. I don't do anything,'" says Weiss. "And then you press: *But surely you moisturize.* And as you peel back that social conditioning around the idea that admitting you have a beauty routine must mean you're frivolous or maybe shouldn't be taken too seriously, you start to realize almost every woman has something to say—'Actually, I've been using this same mascara for ten years, and it's the most amazing product. Let me tell you about it.'"

Weiss wanted to debunk this stigma and erase this shame. To do it, she decided, she'd call upon her magazine training and create a blog. (This, after all, was the era in which blogs were transforming nobodies into style stars.) She sketched out a logo (a blot of nail polish), came up with a few regular features, and spent $700 on a camera and a website built by a friend of a friend. She called it Into the Gloss.

Into the Gloss launched in September 2010 with a post about fashion publicist Nicky Deam and a banner ad from beauty giant Lancôme. The cosmetics brand had explored partnerships with bloggers but struggled to find one that matched its taste level. Then Weiss spent a week pestering its then-PR director, Kerry Diamond, for a meeting. When Weiss finally got in the door, "she opened up her laptop and, like, unicorns and rainbows and sunshine shot out of it—just, like, *wow*," says Diamond. The writing was cultivated but conversational, light but not silly; the graphic design, sophisticated and inviting; and the photography, beautiful. "It was everything we wanted but didn't know we needed," says Diamond. The brand signed on to advertise.

Weiss kept her day job and ran her site every morning between 4 A.M. and 8 A.M. Her audience grew swiftly—a combination of Weiss' appeal and the fact that she produced genuinely compelling content that was often far more revealing and smart and personal than your average beauty coverage. Columns like "The Top Shelf," which she often conducted while sitting on the subject's bathroom floor, featured insider-y interviews in which supermodels, magazine editors, and beauty and fashion execs revealed their daily routines, preferred products and, in a plot twist, quite candid struggles with insecurities (supermodel Karlie Kloss on acne, J. Crew's then-creative director Jenna Lyons on aging and ice cream). Beauty at Into the Gloss became not something that divided women but something that united them, offering a sort of catharsis, companionship, and assurance.

After a year of this, Weiss had amassed ten million page views a month, several successful corporate partnerships, and a small staff. She quit her job at *Vogue* to focus on the site full-time. But she sensed there was a wider audience to reach. Into the Gloss had succeeded in democratizing beauty in a way, but it was still undeniably prestigious.

The women profiled weren't always relatable, zits or no; the products they suggested weren't always readily available or affordable. "That wasn't helping the mission," Weiss recalls, "which was really about creating your own idea of who you want to be and using beauty as just one way to do that."

Which led to her next question: What *would* help the mission?

In 2013, Weiss started approaching venture capitalists with a vague idea about products or maybe an Into the Gloss-curated ecommerce platform. She told them that for three years, she'd been spending her days in conversations with women who had lots to say about what the big beauty brands weren't doing for them. Beauty consumers, she said, were overwhelmed by offerings, and brands weren't helping themselves—"launching the craziest things that aren't user-friendly, or don't really work, or don't help you replace anything," says Weiss. The cabinets under women's sinks, her own included, were full of Ziploc bags of stuff they never used.

Weiss wanted women to have products that would never let them down or see the inside of a Ziploc bag. She was more interested in something being good than being new. But she struggled with what to do next. For one, she didn't have a clear business plan. For another, she was schlepping all over New York talking to "mostly dads" who couldn't appreciate the problem or her simple solution. She didn't have, as she says, "some huge technological advancement or patent that differentiates my beauty product from another person's beauty product." She didn't even have a product, really. She had a mentality.

Still, she kept at it. After ten or so rejections, a meeting at Thrive Capital—which liked what she had to say but told her to come back once she had a product—led Weiss to venture capitalist Kirsten Green, the founder of San Francisco-based Forerunner Ventures. Green needed no convincing. She agreed that there was plenty of room in the $428 billion beauty industry for improvement. "Emily knew nothing about supply chain or customer experience or building a team," Green says. "There were no products, no business plan. But when I saw what she could do on her own with no resources, how compelling she was, I knew I wanted to be in business with this person."

Green helped Weiss raise $2 million in seed funding, which she used to assemble a small team, including creative director Helen Steed, a beauty industry vet who'd helped build Bumble & Bumble, and COO Henry Davis who came from the London office of venture capital firm Index Ventures. Davis was brought on specifically to help turn Weiss' almost unending list of creative ideas into actionable items. "One of Emily's greatest strengths was in recognizing the need for a business partner and charging her staff with the right responsibilities," says Green. "So many entrepreneurs view their companies as their babies. They micromanage, and they stall."

With Davis' help, Weiss settled on launching a product line. She believed she could make a better beauty product with the feedback of her readers. "You don't need most beauty products," she says. "They're an emotional purchase. That's why the conversations are really important. What choice do you have but to ask your customer what they want?" She partnered with a California-based chemist to create an initial line of high-quality basics—essentials that were easy to use, affordable, and encompassed all she'd learned from her readers. For example, a moisturizer that wouldn't cause breakouts, didn't interfere with makeup, wasn't super expensive, and smelled nice: literally what she'd heard women asking for time and time again.

Then, there was price. The beauty industry runs on prestige pricing and equates high cost with high quality. That left a space open for Glossier to make a statement with low pricing. "A dirty little secret of the beauty industry is that Chanel No. 5 costs, like, $150, but to actually make the Chanel No. 5 costs, like, nothing," Weiss says. "Making a bougie, expensive beauty brand wasn't helping the mission or very fun for me. We can all be united by that $12 coconut balm. You don't need to charge an arm and a leg." The packaging was also designed to inspire conversation. Glossier's bottles would be Instagram-worthy, with a lot of white space, and each purchase came with a sheet of emoji-like stickers—leading consumers to personalize their bottles and then share them on social media.

In October 2014, Weiss unveiled the brand's first four products on her blog, along with a note saying it "is the beginning, I hope, of a new way of looking at beauty." When Glossier's site went live at 6 a.m., she and her small team gathered around a single laptop, bleary-eyed from having not gone to sleep, and crossed their fingers. They'd offered a first-day promotion in which New Yorkers who ordered before 2 P.M. could select same-day delivery. The response was overwhelming. "There were, like, 12 people working here," says Weiss. "We were Uber-rushing our first-day deliveries to customers in New York using, like, 30 burner phones. Everyone was doing something that was not their job." Weiss did a few deliveries herself, which Glossier filmed and put on Instagram. It was chaos. Beautiful chaos.

Six weeks after its launch, the company announced $8.4 million in Series A funding led by Thrive Capital. Weiss used the money to invest in technology and data analytics that would study Instagram and other social platforms, measuring not just how well certain Glossier posts performed but how well each product performed: Were people sharing them as product shots, or selfies, or not at all? Which user-generated posts sparked the most engagement, and how much more engaged could they be?

For an entrepreneur who had recently struggled to impress investors without a new technology, Weiss was hitting upon something at once obvious and revolutionary. Her customers lived on social, and her products are visual by design, which meant that, with the right tools in place, sites like Instagram could become Glossier's R&D lab and marketing platform. So first, she ensured that customers would feel heard on Instagram—having her marketing, editorial, and customer service teams take turns responding to all comments publicly or by direct message. (This still happens today.) And then, critically, the company began using Instagram to build mini focus groups and quickly create products based on what they learn. One post in February 2016, for example, asked followers what they wanted most in a heavy-duty moisturizer. More than 1,000 people responded; the company took that feedback and used it to build a product called Priming Moisturizer Rich, which released in January 2017.

This has become the way Glossier now talks with its consumer. It asks, it listens, and it churns out a new product every six to eight weeks—"enough time to get it, use it, shoot it, talk about it, and then you have another one," Weiss says. And this approach has led to furious brand loyalty. Weiss says that 70 percent of online sales and traffic comes through peer-to-peer referrals, a number that's remained constant. Now Glossier is constantly experimenting with how to harness the power of that community to even greater strength. Earlier this year, for example, it launched a program in which more than 420 of its most active and influential community members sell products to their friends and followers; in turn, they receive a cut of the profits as well as rewards that include sneak previews of products and trips to New York to visit Glossier and have dinner with Weiss. By summer, the program had helped generate 7 percent of the brand's annual revenue.

Recently, Glossier also began to dabble in out-of-home advertising with campaigns on the High Line in New York City and on Los Angeles construction barriers. This, too, has gone viral. "Girls take pictures of themselves with the ads and tag us," says Weiss.

"Can you imagine that happening with, like, Ford Motors?"

Weiss did make one big error in how she built her community, though. At first, she underestimated just how engaged it really was. By late 2015, Glossier had amassed several waiting lists for its products—some that made news for reaching 10,000 people long. The problem came to a head in July 2016 when the brand sold a year's worth of inventory in a single month. "We weren't paying for marketing—it was all social-driven—and as a new company, you can guess, but you have no idea what to prepare for," she says. Later, she hired a director of supply chain management from Apple. And with the high number of orders, she was able to fix part of the problem. Her manufacturers were suddenly happy to move a lot faster than before. "At the time, we were *begging* vendors to run 10,000 pieces of something." Weiss smiles. "Once we could say we wanted to order 150,000, they were much more accommodating."

One day in late 2014, Emily Weiss was riding the subway when a woman introduced herself. "She came up to me and said, 'I just love Glossier,'" says Weiss. Weiss asked what the woman did for work. "She said, 'I just graduated college, and I don't have a job.'" As it happened, Weiss was in the market for an assistant. "Come in and interview," she said. The woman did, and she got the job.

After a year, the woman asked to work in product development. "She's 22 and never worked in product development," says Weiss. "But off she went to product development and helped develop four of our best-selling products, including one called Cloud Paint."

Cloud Paint, a cream blush, launched in March 2017. To market it, Weiss hired ten makeup artists to use the blush on celebrity clients attending the Oscars and post the results on social media. Regrams throughout the Glossier community resulted in 1,700 user-generated images over seven days; by week four, there were 6,368 images of Cloud Paint on Instagram. "And I was so excited to be able to email my former assistant—she got married and moved to Sweden, so doesn't even work here anymore—and tell her, 'People love Cloud Paint, those colors are really good, and you did a great job.' And, you know, that was luck—just a girl I met one day on the train."

But then, that's the nature of building an inclusive company. When you listen to everyone, you'll find they all have something valuable to say.

12 COMPANIES DISRUPTING MONEY EXCHANGE

Andrew Medal

From domestic, peer-to-peer transactions to large-scale, international dealings, exchanging money will always be a part of our daily existence. That's what makes this industry so ripe for technological innovation.

Here are 12 companies using technology to disrupt traditional concepts of money exchange to make things faster, cheaper, and more reliable for consumers.

1. Venmo

Venmo embraced a social model of money exchange to target millennials—and it has worked. Part social network, part transaction service, this app operates only on mobile technology and allows people to pay their family and friends with just a phone number or email address. With more than 15 percent of peer-to-peer transactions being used to split bills (according to a 2016 report from Medici)—a common millennial brunch tradition—Venmo's ease of use and mobility have made the app a favorite among younger crowds.

2. TransferWise

Worldwide, about $582 billion was sent by U.S. immigrants to relatives in their home countries in 2015, according to the Pew Research Center. TransferWise recognized this huge market and made it easier for people to make peer-to-peer transactions by charging much less than banks do to exchange funds from one currency to another. With a low 1 percent charge per transaction, the company allows people to cross borders without breaking the bank.

3. Xoom

With the market for peer-to-peer transfers and remittances being worth more than $1 trillion, Xoom has taken mobile functionality to the next level. Now operating as a PayPal service, the company provides fast, simple, and secure ways to send money, reload phone minutes, and pay bills for people around the world.

4. Remitly

Remittances accounted for almost four times the $135 billion in global foreign aid that was disbursed in 2015, according to the World Bank. Remitly, the largest independent digital remittance company in the United States, has certainly contributed to that number. Through its user-friendly mobile app, it allows people of all ages to send money easily and transparently by eliminating the forms, codes, fees, and other aspects of more old-school methods.

5. Apple Pay

The majority of people are starting to give up cash for plastic—there are almost 1.9 billion active credit card accounts in the U.S. Apple Pay has taken this one step further by allowing users to use their smartphones, computers, and wearable devices to pay for everything from in-person retail purchases to online shopping using the Safari browser.

6. CurrencyPay

CurrencyPay is making great strides towards streamlining the online payment process through its greatly expanded payment options. It ensures timely payment to sellers, allows merchants to process high ASP credit card transactions at competitive rates, helps users pay with checks online, offers real-time credit decisions for customers within minutes, and more. The online commerce world is far behind the real world in terms of providing consumers and vendors with flexible payment options. If you don't have a credit card or Paypal, you are out of luck with making purchases online. CurrencyPay changes all that. CurrencyPay gives consumers a lot of options (credit card, debit card, ACH, wire, financing) and the fastest financing process in the world (online or off). It's a real game changer in the world of online payments.

7. Xapo

The average bitcoin market price is more than $2,000, but if you have some lying around or are able to buy it, Xapo has developed a great way to securely store and use your bitcoin funds. The company allows users to purchase bitcoins, manage them with their easy-to-use online wallet, store them in a secure vault, and even spend them with a physical debit card.

8. Paym

With mobile peer-to-peer users in the U.S. expected to grow from 69 million to 126 million by 2020 (according to The Payments Review), Paym (pronounced "pay-em") is making sure that money transaction technology is keeping up with the needs of the 21st century. Allowing users to transfer money using just a phone number, it simplifies the process of both peer-to-peer and peer-to-business transactions.

9. Kantox

It's no secret that forex traders can make a lot of money. In fact, Daily FX reports more than 50 percent of international trades are closed out at a gain. However, there's always more money to be made, and Kantox can help with that. The company provides a marketplace for businesses to exchange currency, which lets them get a much better exchange rate than what's offered by traditional banks and brokers.

10. Get4x

A common complaint about international travel is the lack of price transparency in forex transactions, and with forex turnover exceeding $4 trillion a day, this is a significant problem, according to a report on forex market statistics from FX Pros. Get4x is a currency exchange-rate aggregator platform for travelers that allows users to find and compare money-changer rates so that they get the best deal every time.

11. CurrencyKart

Close to 33 million U.S. residents traveled overseas in 2015, and we're willing to bet that most of them had to exchange their U.S. dollars for local currency. Delhi-based CurrencyKart lets users compare the rates of forex dealers across the country to find the best value. It's similar to Get4x but takes the usage one step further: it allows users to get their forex delivered to their doorstep.

12. RateX

With ecommerce fraud growing more common with overseas transactions—more than 30 percent of Indonesian online purchases are fraudulent, for instance, as reported in 2015 by Forter—it's important that users know their transactions are secure and accurate. RateX, a Google Chrome extension, helps with this by offering real exchange rates without hidden transaction fees. It allows users to pay for an international purchase in local currency to keep things understandable and transparent.

26

HOW THE STARS OF "FIXER UPPER" TRANSFORMED A TEXAS TOWN

Maggie Gordon

One night a few years ago, Dustin Anderson was having dinner with his wife. He spotted Chip and Joanna Gaines out with some friends. Anderson felt immediate tension. He owns a Waco, Texas, glass shop called Anderson Glass and had been doing some work with the Gaineses who owned a construction company. But the Gaineses were past due on paying him—30 or maybe closer to 60 days overdue.

"There was an elephant in the room," Anderson recalls. "We sat down for dinner, and then after a while, Chip walks over and slides into the booth, puts his arm around me, and says, 'Hey, buddy. I know we're behind. Things are rough, but bear with me. I have a solution.' And he just kind of loved on me. When he got up and left, I told my wife, 'That's what I want.' Just talk to me. Tell me. Keep me in the loop.'"

The moment was pure Chip. He's a lovable, charming guy. But he'd also gotten used to conversations like that. Back then, around 2011, Chip and Joanna didn't think they'd make payroll most weeks, as they flipped homes on a shoestring budget. ("It's not like shiplap was always my top design choice," says Joanna. "I was just trying to save money.") Monday and Tuesday would be full of angst as they crunched numbers. Friday would be gut-wrenching when they had to ask employees or contractors to hold checks. "I think it would have been easier to quit if it was just me and Chip," Joanna says now. But many of their employees had worked alongside them for years. "And we had these guys who were now family. We knew their wives; we knew their kids. We were like, 'We can't not do this for them.' Even though they couldn't cash their checks on some Fridays, they were the reason why we were like, 'We've got to make this work.'"

Their fortunes changed in 2013 as any fan of reality television knows. Chip and Joanna became the stars of an HGTV show called *Fixer Upper*, a home-remodeling program in which their loving rapport takes center stage, and it turned them into America's sweethearts. Viewers live-tweet episodes with the hashtag #RelationshipGoals and heart emojis. Now, the Gaineses are building a personal empire: they run the construction and design business (which is booming) and the show (which in 2016 filming of season four wrapped up) alongside their new magazine, *The Magnolia Journal*. ("Magnolia" is the Gaineses' umbrella corporate name. Their construction company, for example, is Magnolia Homes.) Their first book, *The Magnolia Story*, came out in October and became an instant best-seller. Joanna has a line of furniture, and they're considering a second show focusing on her design process.

Reality television has, of course, transformed many such struggling businesspeople before them. But the couple's response to fame has very much separated them from their newly famous peers: they've invested heavily in Waco, a city of 130,000 that's also something of a fixer-upper. In opening multiple businesses there, they've helped turn the city into a certifiable tourist destination—sparking not just an ecosystem of other businesses that serve the tens of thousands of fans rolling in each week but also a model of how entrepreneurs in other cities, even without the backing of a cable TV show, can make an enormous difference.

It's something the Gaineses are proof of: successful entrepreneurs inspire other entrepreneurs, and their collective success is transformative.

"We want Waco to be part of the package, part of the equation," says Chip. "It's become exciting to watch people come to town and go back home and say, 'We had a great time. This place was great.'"

Waco was once booming. In the late-19th and early-20th centuries, it was Texas' major cotton exchange. Today, most people think of it as the stained site of sensational tragedy—the siege that destroyed a cult called the Branch Davidians in 1993—but the city's troubles began long before then. The Great Depression left lasting damage, followed by an F-5 tornado in 1953 that shredded the town like a colossal rogue weed whacker. After that, downtown Waco began to look like a far-flung first cousin of the small, forgotten cities that make up the Northeast's Rust Belt.

The losses kept mounting. In 1964, 5,000 people were out of work when Waco's James Connally Air Force Base closed. Nineteen years later, 1,400 people were out when General Tire Co. shuttered its plant—and left a 300,000-square-foot factory to stand vacant, a symbol of Waco's daunting future. "When I was younger, I couldn't wait to get the hell out of here," says Kristina Collins, senior vice president for economic development at the Greater Waco Chamber of Commerce, who has lived here since the early '90s.

The city did have one potential economic engine: Baylor University, a private Baptist college in the heart of downtown. But like many small cities with big colleges, Waco struggled to keep its freshly educated young people in town. They'd often drive an hour and a half to Dallas or Austin where they'd find better job opportunities and a more vibrant community. Chip and Joanna could have been a part of that common story. Neither grew up in the town they now call home.

Chip was raised in the Dallas-Ft. Worth area and moved to Waco to attend Baylor. He'd considered himself a serial entrepreneur since his teens, and by his sophomore year, he'd launched a business mowing lawns; a wash-and-fold business would follow, and he even experimented with selling firecrackers at a roadside stand. After graduating in 1998, having saved up some cash, he decided to buy and fix up a local house. The profit he made when he sold it six months later was more than he'd made in a year of mowing lawns.

"That's when things started making real sense to me," Chip says. So he did it again, learning as he went. "When I bought the house, the windows were broken, so I had to figure out how to fix windows. The wood floors were rotten, and I had to figure out how to replace hardwood floors. It was a backward way to do it, and I wouldn't recommend it."

The year 2001 brought the meet-cute story that *Fixer Upper* fans are familiar with. Chip had always admired the photo of a pretty girl at his local auto shop—the owner's daughter. Then one day, he went in to get his brakes fixed, and there was the girl: Joanna. She grew up in Austin, but her family moved to Waco when she was a teenager. She is four years younger than Chip and had recently graduated from Baylor herself. Their hashtag-able chemistry sparked and they were married in 2003.

The two wanted to make life work in Waco. They liked living in a small place that was only an hour-and-a-half drive from major cities, should they want a big night out on the town. Joanna opened a home-goods store in 2003 but closed it a few years after so they could both focus on Chip's construction business and their growing family. Joanna became a self-taught interior decorator so she and Chip could work as a team.

By staying in Waco, the Gaineses unwittingly joined a new kind of small-city American story. It goes like this: Local entrepreneur gets serious about saving (or simply improving) the city they love and, with success, becomes the focal point for a bustling business scene that changes the way that city sees itself. "Twenty years ago, the most talented people tried to find their way to New York, Boston, and San Francisco," says Weston Wamp, principal of Lamp Post Ventures in Chattanooga. "And some people still do that. But now, because of the way the world works, anyone in any sector can do it in any place of their choosing." Case in point: Lamp Post operates a venture capital fund that lures companies from the coast to the often overlooked core of America, including Chattanooga, a city that used to lose young professionals to nearby Atlanta and Nashville. Lamp Post is now transforming an old hotel into tiny apartments for all the new startup types it has lured there.

Among the top ten most expensive U.S. cities, 51.1 percent of people moving out are 18 to 34, according to Trulia, a rate significantly higher than that of average migration. Sometimes, these millennials are just moving to the suburbs to start families. Other times, they're headed to places where somebody has sparked an entrepreneurial fire.

The igniter can take all forms, and it doesn't have to involve couples made famous by reality television. In Greenville, South Carolina, it's a small-business incubator. In Baltimore, it's a craft-brewing incubator and Under Armour. In Madison, Wisconsin, it's companies like Epic, the largest healthcare IT company in the country. "Epic started up with a handful of people, and now they have, like, 8,000 employees," says Bill McMeekin, an editor at Livability.com, a site that promotes small- and medium-size cities, who sees stories like this one all the time. "Those employees are leaving and starting their own companies and doing that in Madison, creating a really vibrant scene."

Building that scene in Waco wasn't easy going. Both Chip and Joanna had a lot to learn, and they leaned on others in the community. That's how Chip first met Dustin Anderson, the glass contractor: "He said to me, 'You're the guy who knows the field. Tell me what I need,'" Anderson says. "Chip learned his craft that way. He listened to the guys who were experts." In the forensic dissection of why an entrepreneur stays in a community, such moments cannot be overestimated. Local businesses in a small city like Waco are often collaborative; they know they need each other to succeed. "We've had so many times when we didn't know if it was going to work—if we were going to make it," says Chip. "More of those than not," Joanna chimes in. "We could cry when we think about the people who held their checks without us knowing it for four weeks. These people wanted us to make it, and we were wanting us to make it. It was like this family effort, and so looking back now, without their effort, we don't know how we would have been able to do it."

But they kept at it, and pure luck struck in the biggest of ways. In 2012, an HGTV producer came upon Joanna's blog where she wrote about projects and home life with Chip. The producer liked Chip and Joanna's authenticity and set up some test shoots with them. Network execs swooned when they saw the footage and soon ordered up one season of the show that would become *Fixer Upper*.

The pilot aired in 2013, and demand for Chip's craftsmanship and Joanna's design sense soared along with their name recognition. It was an odd kind of fame. They hadn't switched jobs, learned acting, moved to Hollywood, or done anything, really, other than what they were already doing—but now with cameras rolling. Maybe this would have happened to them in any town; it's impossible to know. But it happened here with the people they'd known for years. They saw Waco as a natural part of their success.

On a Thursday in October of 2017, Joanna is where she usually is: hunkered down in her office. While many of the homes she designs on TV are staged with whitewashed or pale shiplap walls, three of her office walls are black and one is yellow. The room looks like a Pinterest page come to life—full of breezy quotes pinned to the wall ("It's not the load that breaks you down, it's the way you carry it")— and, today, a summertime candle from her home collection is turning the air bright with citrus. Her designers parade through in 30-minute blocks, one after another to present her with design options for the seemingly endless supply of projects on deck—a new restaurant, a potential home for season five, a prospective vacation rental, and so on.

As she works with her senior project manager, Kristen Bufton, sorting through choices for exterior lighting on an upcoming renovation, Joanna hears Chip's voice boom through the walls as he tells a story a few rooms away, and she pauses.

"So loud. So long-winded," she says, turning to face the direction his voice is traveling from. She smiles. "I love it."

Chip is working on separate projects. Right now, he is in the upstairs portion of their office space balancing calls with the network and meetings with their real estate firm. In the years since the TV show began, the Gaineses have regularly increased their stake in Waco. The show certainly does some of the heavy lifting. It features local contractors like Anderson, which helps those businesses, and the homes the Gaineses flip sometimes become hot Airbnb attractions. Earlier this year, they bought a historic restaurant just outside downtown. When they saw a story in the local newspaper about another small-business owner seeking donations to open a grocery store in low-income North Waco, which has been dubbed a food desert, they held an auction to raise money for the cause.

"We don't want to end up stupid rich while a bunch of people are trying to make ends meet," says Chip. "We want everyone to be on the opposite side of this decades from now, looking back and saying, 'Hey, our lives are better because of us taking that leap of faith.'"

The city has clearly factored that into its plans.

Chip and Joanna's business, to be clear, is not the only thing going in Waco. In 2009, that old tire factory—the one that closed in 1985—was donated to Baylor and slowly became the Baylor Research and Innovation Collaborative, a place to provide budding entrepreneurs with resources to help build their companies. Now fully open, Baylor cites research showing that for every job created at a research park like this, 2.57 jobs are created elsewhere—often in local, emerging industries. "We're designed specifically to keep people here," says Truell Hyde, vice provost for research at Baylor and the center's director.

But Waco also knows the reach the Gaineses have and has given them the tools to expand. In 2014, it provided $208,376 in tax incentives for the couple to transform a 2.6-acre site, including a 20,000-square-foot barn, into what Joanna calls "an amusement park for adults." With HGTV cameras rolling, they rebuilt the place as Magnolia Market at the Silos—a sprawling space with a home-goods store, a garden, a bakery, space for food trucks, and open space to lounge and play yard games. They also own a nearby vacation rental home called The Magnolia House, where visitors can stay for $695 to $995 a night.

Today, white-sneakered visitors pour from a tour bus, phones at the ready to capture a photo sure to make their Facebook friends jealous. The place now attracts more than 20,000 tourists a week. The couple stops by when they can—even in a city this small, they're now often too busy—and sometimes run into unexpected visitors.

"Chip would get into people's cars—he still does this—and ask if they want a picture with him. And he's out there doing that and then, all of a sudden, Laura Bush is there," Joanna says, laughing.

It turns out, the former First Lady is a fan.

"She's come to the Silos a couple times," says Joanna.

"I don't mean to brag, but I'd call her a mega-fan," Chip offers.

"No," Joanna chides him, trying to keep a straight face.

But Chip is on a roll. "I'd say stalker."

"Stop." Joanna is using her mom voice now.

"Mega-fan," Chip tosses out before the subject is changed on him.

Laura Bush's level of fandom aside, the city's chamber of commerce is certainly a mega-fan. "What Magnolia has done has also spurred a lot of other businesses," says Collins, the chamber of commerce executive who once wanted to flee her hometown. "Our downtown is going through a renaissance right now—a complete rebirth." The Gaineses' project has spawned a design district that appeals to tourists, sure, but also a growing band of locals. Between 2011 and 2014, downtown Waco's 76701 zip code's population grew by 32 percent—a deluge compared with the current annual American growth rate of less than 1 percent. Its largest gains are in residents between the ages of 25 and 34. Now, more restaurants, bars, and other businesses are popping up to support these new people. There's even a renewed focus on improving downtown's parks.

And no one is waiting to cash the Gaineses' checks.

When Joanna met Chip, the two worked at different speeds. Joanna preferred to focus on one thing at a time. Chip wanted to run multiple businesses and flip multiple houses at once. It's clear which partner influenced the other. "If we just have one house, we're bored with that," Joanna says now. "So I think Chip has taught me—or has rubbed off on me—but it's, like, the busier, the better. We like to stay busy, and I think we love to stay inspired, and that's the best place for us to be."

Their shared insatiable appetite to keep going— to keep building and to make Waco a destination— has another side. In a short time, Waco has faced a lot of change. And the reality is, change can be hard.

When the *Fixer Upper* pilot aired in 2013, the median home value in Waco was $96,102, according to Trulia. By 2016, it had increased to $110,254—up 14 percent. That's still much more affordable than the median price in the U.S., which rings in at $187,000. But this kind of increase can easily affect up-and-comers' ability to buy a place of their own. And even those who have already bought in saw big issues this year, when property assessments went up by as much as 50 percent. The Gaineses can't possibly have caused all this, of course, but people around town often call it a *Fixer Upper* side effect.

"There's been a tremendous amount of redevelopment in the downtown area, and the fact that you have all these visitors coming in caused property values to skyrocket and taxes to rise as a result," says Collins. "And there were a lot of concerns with that because we don't want to stifle the growth and either force the people who have invested out because they can't afford to pay their taxes or make it cost-prohibitive for new people to come in."

Small cities that have yet to find their own Chip and Joanna might call this a nice problem to have. But it's also a problem that could solve someone else's problem. If Waco becomes too expensive, say, the next Chip and Joanna might move somewhere even smaller and start the whole cycle again.

27

THIS DESIGNER BUCKED FASHION NORMS. LEARN WHY IT WORKED.

Stephanie Schomer

Consumers have more information at their fingertips than ever. Ecommerce has changed how people shop. And yet many industry traditions have remained—like, say, fashion's longstanding insistence that brands create four collections a year. But even the most deeply embedded rules are starting to crack. Tanya Taylor is one of the changemakers. She's a fashion designer who remade her schedule to focus on just two strong collections a year—which in turn will spend more time on the retail floor rather than being relegated to the sale section to make room for an impending pre-collection. Taylor tells us how she bucked expectations . . . and why it worked out.

Entrepreneur: You launched in 2012 with two collections a year and in 2015 expanded to four: resort and prefall in addition to spring and fall. But this year, you canceled resort. Why?

Taylor: When we expanded, I immediately noticed the pressure the extra collections put on our very small team without ever really producing a valuable outcome. This summer, we were working on resort 2017, and I just didn't feel inspired. What if I could take my energy and put it toward something I really did care about? So I told our team we were canceling the collection, which is a weird conversation to have about something you're already working on! They thought something was wrong, but I was like, "No, this is a good thing." It was a great reset.

Entrepreneur: How did your retail partners react?

Taylor: I was nervous that we would lose their trust, but overwhelmingly, they came out for our spring/summer appointments with a fresh level of enthusiasm. Our precollections were never as strong in sell-throughs. So the extra time let us consider how to really strengthen our main collection.

Entrepreneur: What did you do differently with your main collection this past season?

Taylor: We partnered with Saks Fifth Avenue; they came in early and saw sketches and fabrics of our spring/summer 2017 collection and purchased 15 styles in advance—which is larger than our entire resort order would have been. When we had our show for Fashion Week, those 15 styles went live on Saks' home page and were immediately available for purchase. Brands pay hundreds of thousands of dollars to be on the home page of Saks, but this partnership cost us nothing.

Entrepreneur: That "see now, buy now" trend is one that more designers are exploring rather than asking customers to wait six months to buy them. How has the industry responded?

Taylor: The industry is extremely supportive of disruption, especially by young designers finding what works for them. Earlier this year, the Council of Fashion Designers of America commissioned a study with the Boston Consulting Group examining the future of New York Fashion Week, and the finding was ultimately to do what's best for your brand! Our product, for example, is emotional, colorful, and print-based. Our customer buys if they think it's great-timing and the seasonal structure aren't as much of a factor for them.

Entrepreneur: You recently ditched runway shows in favor of presentations [where models stand stationary as editors and buyers move about the full collection]. What was behind that decision?

Taylor: When we launched, we started with presentations. It felt really right for us. But there's a natural progression where you think runway is what you do when you grow—and so we did runway. And I missed being out on the floor, talking to editors and getting immediate feedback. Reverting to presentations, everyone kind of looks at you wondering why you would go back to where you started. But when we returned to presentations for 2016, our sales almost doubled. It's what made sense for us, and that's how we have to keep moving forward.

ENTREPRENEUR VOICES SPOTLIGHT: INTERVIEW WITH NICOLE SAHIN AND DEBBIE MILLIN

Nicole Sahin is founder and CEO of Globalization Partners, and Debbie Millin is COO.

If you truly want to learn the secrets to seriously hacking growth, a great case study wouldn't focus on a company that's inherently scalable—say, a digital product or mass-manufacturing. Digital products have their own challenges, to be sure, but going from a hundred users to a thousand isn't that big of a leap. Mass-manufacturing requires capital, engineering, and infrastructure, but it's designed around the idea of mass production.

No, a great case study would look at an industry inherently *un*scalable, and then find a company that's experienced phenomenal growth *despite* that.

Cue Globalization Partners.

The company went from an idea with no outside capital in 2012 to an astounding $40 million in annual revenue with barely 20-something employees just four short years later. Doing what, you ask? Primarily by providing a legal platform to enable companies to engage their global workforce without having to deal with complex legal, tax, and HR issues in each locale.

That's right: they growth hacked global HR.

Founder and CEO Nicole Sahin with COO Debbie Millin share the secrets to Globalization Partners' envy-inspiring success.

Entrepreneur: Globalization Partners has an amazing story. Not only was it recently ranked as one of Inc. 500's top ten fastest-growing private companies, it has redefined its industry.

Sahin: Thank you. Yes, we are quite proud of what we've accomplished in just a few years. We are currently the only true PEO [professional employer organization] and employer-of-record in over 150 countries with its own legal platform covering more than 85 percent of the market.

But when I founded Globalization Partners, growing as quickly as possible was not my vision. Growth was not the only goal, nor was disrupting our industry; they've just been byproducts of our business model.

What I'm most proud of is being recognized by *Inc.* as one of the best workplaces to work in America and by the Global Payroll Awards as "PEO of the Year." Those are the accolades we want. If we experience exponential growth and yet hate coming to work, frustrate our clients and partners, and spend our days putting out one fire after another, what have we really achieved?

Millin: What Nicole is speaking to is Globalization Partners' culture. Nicole's superpower is to find that magic blend of achieving high performance while ensuring that people love working with us. That focus on culture provides the platform that enables everything else from workflow to technology rollouts to taking care of our clients. While we're happy to share some of our tactics and decisions that have led to a high-growth company, none of it would matter without Nicole's unwavering commitment to a wonderful workplace environment and relentless focus on keeping our clients happy.

Entrepreneur: I love that you attribute your phenomenal growth directly to company culture. Often, startup entrepreneurs see it as an "either-or" problem. You can have a high-growth, high-pressure startup or you can love coming to work; you can't have both. Your example turns that thinking on its head. What's another high-level strategy that's substantially contributed to the company's growth?

Sahin: I know it might sound boring, but I'll talk first about recurring revenue. To successfully build a scalable business, you need to build it around sustainable processes. When you have an element of recurring revenue, you have a number you can rely on and plan for. It's hard to plan for a future you can't predict with at least some confidence. I've seen many entrepreneurs try to plan their businesses out, but their revenue stream is entirely project- or service-based. You can't plan for tomorrow's growth when you don't know if money's even going to be coming through the door.

Millin: That key idea—planning ahead—is probably one of the most important things that has allowed us to scale. In being profiled for the women business leadership book *Disrupters*, author Dr. Patti Fletcher pointed out that most high-growth entrepreneurs try to build the plane while flying it. Nicole spent a year laying the foundation for Globalization Partners before she launched the company.

That kind of thinking has led our leadership team to look as far down the road as possible, to realistically plan for the future, and to build what the business needs before it even arrives at that point. Instead of fixing problems as they arise, we want to identify the bottlenecks as far ahead of time as we can and plan around them.

We don't "cross that bridge when we get there" because the bridge that's there might not hold us. Instead, we build our own bridge ahead of time so that we know exactly how the crossing will go.

Entrepreneur: So far, neither of you have talked about the role of tech.

Sahin: You cannot underestimate what technology allows. It's part of the mantra of "people, process, and technology" that all executives chant. Yet there have been countless times when I need to sign a legal document sent by another company and I'll tell the person, "Can you send it to me by DocuSign?" and they'll say, "No, we don't use it. It's too expensive: it's $25 per user per month!" So instead, they make their executives spend a half-hour printing something, signing it by hand, scanning it, and then attaching it by email. That's absolutely stupid.

But those little timesavers are peanuts compared to what you can achieve by really investing in your own technology—which is one of the biggest impacts Millin has had. When she first came on board, there were only seven of us, so we didn't have to be particularly advanced, but I wanted to stay ahead of the curve and have tech enable our growth—not hinder it.

Millin: We created a proprietary software system for Globalization Partners. Thousands of entrepreneurs, managers, and consultants have horror stories about just implementing enterprise-wide software changes, much less designing and creating a custom one.

But here again, the culture of Globalization Partners enabled the process. We say that three months here is like a year anywhere else because of how fast-paced we move. Our team is used to adapting quickly. We've made open and effective communication part of how we operate. Every new hire starts with our weeklong course we jokingly named "GPU," which exposes each person to every aspect of the business from sales and marketing to finance and operations; everybody starts with a working knowledge of what everyone else does.

We had tons of communication, testing, and feedback, resulting in a system tailor-made for our workflows within each team and between all our departments. We have a tech platform that will work not just for a year or two but for Globalization Partners' foreseeable future. That investment has put us far ahead of our competitors and given us unmatched agility and capability.

Entrepreneur: What's been a hard lesson during all of this, especially in regard to how it hurt your growth? Put another way: what could you have done differently to have grown even faster?

Sahin: One aspect that has been extremely challenging for me, both emotionally and cognitively, is recognizing when the business has outgrown an employee. There were times when someone who was formerly a rock star employee no longer was. I would ask myself, *How have they changed? What are they doing differently than they were six months ago?*

It took me some time before realizing that that person hadn't changed at all; the role had simply surpassed their skillset or their superpower that we needed so much when we hired them. The thing is, nobody's going to come knocking on your door to say, "Nicole, I think this job has outgrown me." Because they are an awesome, ambitious go-getter, they're going to try to do a great job. But as they become more overwhelmed, as things begin moving too quickly for them and they feel more disorganized, they become discouraged. Eventually, they stop being able to competently function.

I had to recognize that reality, then start trying to correct it. Those are very difficult conversations to have: the person may have done a great job in the past, but they aren't capable of doing a great job anymore. It's even more difficult to try to get ahead of that problem. But the longer it goes, the bigger of an issue it becomes. In hindsight, I just wish I would have seen those instances for what they were sooner.

Millin: I think of Jim Collins' metaphor about having the right people on the bus and in the right seats. In a high-growth business, if the bus has a flat, you have to change it while the bus is still going 100 miles an hour. We have some people I think of as utility players because they're versatile; we can plug them into different roles as needed and they can quickly adapt to it. One thing we've learned is to be flexible in gauging talent. Sometimes, we'll think we need someone with experience for a certain position but then discover that having someone less experienced allows them to be more flexible because they don't have certain expectations about a role.

So my experience echoes Nicole's: getting the right people and putting them in the right place has probably been the hardest lesson to learn, and it's an issue that you have to continue to assess and address.

Entrepreneur: What's one counterintuitive piece of advice you'd give concerning growth hacking?

Sahin: The typical business model in our industry is to subcontract PEO services to an in-country company. Say you wanted to open a regional office in Mexico. You would contact a company like Globalization Partners. They would turn around and contact their counterpart in Mexico who would actually hire and onboard your employees there.

On paper, that makes sense. It's not feasible for a U.S.-based PEO to have in-country operations in every nation on the planet. That's not scalable. It's easier to have preferred partners. At least, that's the conventional thinking.

In reality, when you do that, you're giving up your supply chain. You're ceding control of your deliverables to dozens of companies who don't do business like you. What happens when they're not built for scale and they start falling apart? What happens if one of your competitors buys them out? What happens when they cost you clients, business, and revenue?

While we started our business this way, we ultimately realized that the most scalable way to stay at the top of this industry was to build those operations in-house. We have Globalization Partner operations covering about 85 percent of the workforce we hire on behalf of our clients globally, and that number will increase to about 95 percent by the end of the year.

We own our supply chain. Instead of outsourcing those bottlenecks for someone else to run into, we rely on our own capabilities to solve them ourselves. The level of legal, tax, and corporate structure skills we've brought onto our in-house team in order to provide this level of quality to our clients is exceptional, but we know that "the obstacle is the path," as we often say. While this has been one of the greatest challenges of building our global business, it makes our lives easier, our clients happier, and (our) net profits higher. We are on a continual quest to break down barriers to global business and are exhilarated at the opportunity the future holds.

WHEN COOKIE DOUGH ACCIDENTALLY GOES VIRAL

Kristen Tomlan

I thought I was ready to open my first brick-and-mortar business. I'd been selling gourmet cookie dough online for two years, and although I knew retail would be an adjustment, I was excited to learn on the job. I believed that we all must go after what we want without hesitation—because if we wait for that "perfect" moment, we'll be waiting forever. And yet, when I opened my shop, DŌ, in Manhattan in January 2017, I was still stunned by just how thoroughly unprepared I was. It was a mess. A disaster. An embarrassment, on occasion—and exciting, scary, wonderful, and terrible at the same time.

And yet, I'll be honest: I wouldn't have it any other way.

It all started with a Facebook video from Insider Food that went viral (with 63 million views). And that led to big crowds—way bigger than we expected. We were grateful for them but unable to serve them the way we'd have wanted to. We ran out of product, we worked overtime to make up for our shortage, and then we ran out of ingredients. Meanwhile, customers were stuck waiting up to five hours for their cookie dough. We didn't have the equipment we needed to produce the quantity of product we needed. Our online orders were pinging in at one order per minute, so we had to shut down online ordering just to keep our heads above the water.

There were only ten of us—five full-time employees and five part-time employees—and we were all beyond exhausted, forcing smiles just to get through the day. When, or rather *if*, we finally got to go home at night, we found that we were just far too stressed to get any degree of rest. At one point, I even called in my family, begging them to fly out from the Midwest as reinforcements. I was desperate.

But, of course, my family couldn't save me from this madness. I could only save myself. So once the initial shock wore off, I began fixing the problem and, for the first time, truly building a business that could achieve what I wanted it to achieve. Here were three big steps I took:

1. I Hired a Lot More Staff

When we ran out of product the first weekend and had to close for two days to get caught up, I used every possible moment I could to post job listings, look at resumes, conduct interviews, and hire all positions— front of house, back of house, and a far larger management team that would include a marketing and social media manager, a dedicated ecommerce team, a director of events, a production manager, a strategic partnership manager, a special project coordinator, and a general manager for the shop.

When evaluating potential new hires, I didn't care as much about prior experience as I did about personality. Scooping cookie dough is teachable. An outgoing, spunky, upbeat personality is not. It was important that I chose like-minded individuals that immediately understood—and bought into—what we had going on here. In a matter of a month, I hired 60 additional employees.

Not every new employee was a winner, and we lost a few of the existing team that couldn't handle the craziness. But that was all just part of the process. We also put necessary policies and procedures in place; got new HR, payroll, and scheduling software to keep it all straight; and re-organized our storage area to accommodate a few desks.

2. I Quickly Increased Production

When I was just selling online, I operated out of a tiny old kitchen. When we signed a ten-year lease on our retail space, we thought we would be able "grow into" it over the years. Ha! After two weeks, we were already out of space. Our kitchen is only 375 square feet, and our product is perishable. Where would we store it all? How could we keep up?

With the new people I hired, we began running three shifts in the kitchen and in the front of house. Production was running 5 A.M. to midnight with a cleaning crew from midnight to 3 A.M. We bought bigger mixers, quadrupled both our refrigerated and frozen storage capacity (which included dropping enormously heavy refrigerators ten feet down through a hole in the sidewalk that led to our basement), and delegated certain portions of production to specific individuals so each person had a distinct task and a distinct responsibility.

But that still wasn't enough. So, we quickly identified potential production partners and larger commissary space in the Bronx. We scaled up our ingredients, trained another new team, and got new containers and new ingredients delivered as quickly as possible. Five weeks after we opened the shop, our new facility was up and running in the Bronx.

3. I Successfully Tracked Inventory Management

The first weekend, when we ran out of ingredients, I ordered double for the following weekend. And we still ran out. So I doubled it again, and we still went through it all—leading me to schlep to the store to purchase more butter and vanilla myself. It was a joke. Ordering, lead times, and minimums were all a learning curve.

So we sat down and analyzed our sales. How many containers and what sizes of containers were we using? If we sold X number of scoops, that was how much dough? How many batches? What was the flavor breakdown, so we could figure out how much of each ingredient we needed each week? What about the spoons and the napkins and the lids and the trash bags? There were so many things we were ordering and from so many vendors. Things got missed.

Then, our suppliers ran out. We were purchasing their entire warehouse stock faster than they could replenish. So we identified new suppliers and backup vendors and begged people to waive minimums—even sometimes going to random far-off warehouses to pick items up to avoid the delivery time. We ordered more of *everything*—our heat-treated flour that is only produced once a month, our containers that take 12 weeks from China. We ordered it all, and this time, more than we thought we would ever need.

Should I have figured out some of these things *before* launching the business? Sure. And if I'd launched a business before, maybe I'd have known to do them. But, I still agree with Reid Hoffman that it's good to be embarrassed by your first product. It means that you put something out into the world that people could react to—and then could change to their liking. I've learned what a wonderful resource of inspiration and information our customers make, and we really try to take their requests and suggestions into account. We relaunched our online sales because of customer demand, and now we ship across the country. We launch two new flavors every month and have the capacity to make specialty items and custom treats. That's all stuff that I might not have done if I hadn't let the public into our process.

Today, DŌ continues to grow. We're partnering with Citi Field, Dylan's Candy Bar, and the Governor's Ball Music Festival, just to name a few. And yet I'm sure that, in five or ten years' time, I'll look back at what I'm doing today, smack my forehead, and be embarrassed about some other part of the business. But that's fine. I know now that, in business, you just have to take the leap, try your hardest, roll with the punches, and figure it out along the way.

SOULJA BOY—THE ORIGINAL GROWTH HACKER

Andrew Medal

Growth hacking is an interesting concept and has helped many startups surpass initial hurdles and become successful. Some people love growth hacking. Others hate it.

All of your favorite tech titans have growth teams, from Facebook to Instagram to Snapchat. The term was supposedly first coined by Sean Ellis back in 2010, but people have been growth hacking long before the term was coined. In fact, one of the most well-known growth hackers is Soulja Boy, who built his career from scratch through clever digital strategies.

Traditional corporate marketing is focused on building on what's already there. Marketers use a number of techniques to expand audiences, build a strategy for long-term results, brand themselves, generate press, etc. While these steps are necessary and valuable in an established business, they don't work well for new ventures that have virtually no presence at all. In the early days of the startup, marketers need to focus on growth . . . and they have no tools, recognition, branding, or industry presence to fall back on.

Growth hackers are hyper-focused on growth and building a brand. While traditional marketers will also focus on it, they don't dedicate most of their time and energy on it. For them, growth isn't the sole focus because they have other goals to meet as well. This strong focus on growth has created a number of strategies and techniques that just didn't work with traditional marketing.

Soulja Boy burst onto the hip-hop scene in an unconventional way. The world first came to know of him when his break-out single, "Crank That," was officially released in September 2007. It reached the number-one spot on the U.S. Billboard chart. This story sounds very similar to other break-out stars. They get noticed by a label, release a hit song, and suddenly, they are everywhere.

Soulja Boy's story is somewhat different because he wasn't really discovered by a label. The rapper had already established a solid online presence and following before his breakout single. He recorded a number of songs in a home studio with a $200 mic and an old computer. He uploaded his songs to a website called SoundClick and sold the songs for 99 cents. Half of the proceeds from the sales went to SoundClick. Despite that, he earned around $10,000 a day.

When MySpace launched, he migrated to that platform and started to build a following there as well. After he created "Crank That," he uploaded it to MySpace for downloads under the name of different popular artists such as 50 Cent, Britney Spears, etc. People would download the song assuming that it was by those popular artists but would instead get his song.

In a 2016 video interview with VLAD TV, he said, "They'd be like, 'What's this shit? This ain't 50, this ain't Britney.' *Then* they would start feeling the song."

Soulja Boy developed a large following and quickly gained the necessary ground swell that he needed to make the industry take notice. This was well before the time of established YouTube celebrities. He was the first artist to sell more than 3 million digital copies of his music and is recognized as the digital trailblazer for hip-hop. His growth hacking techniques made him fast money, established his brand, and changed the way artists entered the industry.

Soulja Boy's strategies wouldn't work today, but that misses the point. The takeaway is that nobody did it the way he did it. He found a way around the established business model using techniques other artists wouldn't even consider, much less use. Because he had no money, no resources, and no experience, he couldn't go the usual route. He had to use hacks to find success.

That's why entrepreneurs and smaller companies are more likely to use growth hacks. It's not just that a certain tool is cool and new. It's that they don't have many other options other than going head-to-head with the big corporate guns. In larger companies, decisions are often made according to the least common denominator. They want to play it safe. Using something untested, unproven, and unconventional gets voted down.

But innovation happens at the edges. You're not going to disrupt your industry by playing it safe.

You're not going to experience ten times the growth by doing the same thing everyone else is doing. You're not going to become a legend by placing the safe bet.

If you want to grow, you've got to be willing to take a risk—to look foolish, to be comfortable with the unknown, to be fine with failure. Soulja Boy didn't find his growth hacks because he wanted to be cool. He found them because he had no other choice. It was get big or go home.

Necessity is the mother of invention. How badly do you need to grow?

PART IV
HACKING YOUR INDUSTRY FOR GROWTH—REFLECTIONS

This is perhaps the most interesting section of the whole book. From a cookie dough entrepreneur to a global HR platform to a legendary rapper—they all figured out how to growth hack their business (though whether by chance or choice is still something of a question in some cases).

But perhaps the most common thread that connects all of these inspiring stories is one of next-level innovation. These growth hacking heroes don't necessarily focus on doing more, but they focus on doing it better and harnessing the power of being different. You, too, can do that—play to your company's strengths to find your unique growth niche.

As we come to the close of this book, you may feel overwhelmed: There are so many things that you could or should be doing. So many things to consider. So many ideas to plan and execute.

But as you get ready to growth hack your business, ask yourself: Are you just doing more because you think it's what you're supposed to do? Or are you doing it because it's what your business needs you to do?

Start growth hacking . . . the right way.

RESOURCES

(In Order of Appearance)

Thank you to our talented Entrepreneur contributors whose content is featured in this book. Below are links to the original articles as they first appeared on Entrepreneur.com. For more information about these contributors, including author bios, visit us at www.entrepreneur.com.

1. Andrew Medal, "What it Takes to Be a Growth Hacker," *Entrepreneur*, February

28, 2017, www.entrepreneur.com/article/289783.

2. Matthew Capala, "5 Growth-Hacking Myths for Software Entrepreneurs," *Entrepreneur*, January 5, 2017, www.entrepreneur.com/article/253889.

3. Neil Patel, "The Entrepreneur's Guide to Hiring a Kickass Growth Hacker," *Entrepreneur*, March 9, 2017, www.entrepreneur.com/article/254751.

4. Andrew Leonard, "Reid Hoffman: To Successfully Grow A Business, You Must 'Expect Chaos'," *Entrepreneur*, April 24, 2017, www.entrepreneur.com/article/292749.

5. Yaov Vilner, "What I Learned From Mentoring Startups in the World's Best Accelerators," *Entrepreneur*, February 21, 2017, www.entrepreneur.com/article/287400.

6. Marty Fukuda, "Successfully Orchestrate the Expansion of a Growing Company," *Entrepreneur*, January 12, 2015, www.entrepreneur.com/article/241660.

7. Per Bylund, "Why You Should Ignore the Success of Facebook and Uber," *Entrepreneur*,

February 6, 2017, www.entrepreneur.com/
article/286488.

8. Brett Relander, "How Growth Hacking Is Redefining Marketing," *Entrepreneur*, January 27, 2015, www.entrepreneur.com/article/242034.

9. Eric Siu, "Is Growth Hacking Right for Your Company?" *Entrepreneur*, April 29, 2014, www.entrepreneur.com/article/233468.

10. Raad Mobrem, "Why Growth Hacking Won't Work for Every Company," *Entrepreneur*, March 20, 2014, www.entrepreneur.com/article/232353.

11. Sujan Patel, "Growth Hack Strategies Any Business Can Use," *Entrepreneur*, November 28, 2016, www.entrepreneur.com/article/283886.

12. Thomas Smale, "5 Growth-Hacking Secrets for Your SaaS Business," *Entrepreneur*, May 18, 2017, www.entrepreneur.com/article/275896.

13. Steve Young, "5 Growth-Hacking Strategies to Increase Your App Downloads," *Entrepreneur*, February 5, 2017, www.entrepreneur.com/article/269497.

14. Abdullahi Muhammed, "Six Growth Hacking Tips for Content Marketers," *Entrepreneur*, August 9, 2017, www.entrepreneur.com/article/280442.

15. Neil Patel, "6 Growth Hack Techniques You Can Try Today," *Entrepreneur*, January 6, 2015, www.entrepreneur.com/article/241142.

16. Sujan Patel, "7 Things to Outsource Immediately to Scale Your Business," *Entrepreneur*, April 10, 2017, www.entrepreneur.com/article/287143.

17. Lydia Belanger, "When This Company Stopped Selling Directly, Its Customer Base Increased by 700 Percent," *Entrepreneur*, July 31, 2017, www.entrepreneur.com/article/297934.

18. Adam Elder, "What Small Brands Do That Big Names Can't," *Entrepreneur*, November 30, 2016, www.entrepreneur.com/article/285533.

19. Per Bylund, "3 Entrepreneurial Lessons from the Amazon-Whole Foods Mega-Merger," *Entrepreneur*, July 6, 2017, www.entrepreneur.com/article/296810.

20. Michel Koopman, "10 Steps to Forming Long-Lasting Strategic Partnerships," *Entrepreneur*,

April 2, 2015, www.entrepreneur.com/article/244539.

21. Gerard Adams, "Relationships Are What Leverage Hard Work Into Success," *Entrepreneur*, November 11, 2016, www.entrepreneur.com/article/284688.

22. Jess Ekstrom, "Why You Should Focus on 'Different' and 'Better,' Not 'More'," *Entrepreneur*, February 25, 2017, www.entrepreneur.com/article/269595.

23. Jaclyn Trop, "How Dollar Shave Club's Founder Built a $1 Billion Company That Changed the Industry," *Entrepreneur*, March 28, 2017, www.entrepreneur.com/article/290539.

24. Alyssa, Giacobbe, "How Glossier Hacked Social Media to Build A Cult-Like Following," *Entrepreneur*, August 15, 2017, www.entrepreneur.com/article/298014.

25. Andrew Medal, "12 Companies That Are Disrupting Money Exchange," *Entrepreneur*, July 18, 2017, www.entrepreneur.com/article/297300.

26. Maggie Gordon, "How the Stars of 'Fixer Upper' Transformed a Town in Texas,"

Entrepreneur, November 28, 2016, www. entrepreneur.com/article/285525.

27. Stephanie Schomer, "This Designer Bucked Fashion Norms. Learn Why It Worked." *Entrepreneur*, November 30, 2016, www. entrepreneur.com/article/285540.

28. Kristen Tomlan, "When This Cookie Dough Company Went Viral, Its Founder Had to Change Everything," *Entrepreneur*, May 30, 2017, www.entrepreneur.com/ article/295004.

29. Andrew Medal, "Soulja Boy Is the OG Growth Hacker," *Entrepreneur*, December 16, 2016, www.entrepreneur.com/article/286605.

Reader's Notes

_____

_____

_____

_____

_____

_____

_____

_____

_____

_____

_____

_____

_____

_____

_____

_____

_____

Reader's Notes

_____

_____

_____

_____

_____

_____

_____

_____

_____

_____

_____

_____

_____

_____

_____

_____

_____

_____

Reader's Notes